GW00601124

ERIC KRIEGER

GOOD OLD SOCCER

THE GOLDEN AGE OF FOOTBALL PICTURE POSTCARDS

Longman London and New York

Longman Group Limited
Longman House, Burnt Mill, Harlow
Essex CM20 2JE, England
Associated companies throughout the world

*Published in the United States of America
by Longman Inc., New York*

First published 1983

British Library Cataloguing in Publication Data
Krieger, Eric
    Good old soccer.
    1. Postal cards – Great Britain – History
    2. Soccer in art
    I. Title
    769'.49796334   NC1878.A/

    ISBN 0 582 40621 8

Library of Congress Cataloging in Publication Data
Krieger, E. (Eric)
    Good old soccer.
    Includes index.
    1. Soccer – history. 2. Postal cards. I. Title.
GV942.5.K74   1983   769'.49796334   83-9893
ISBN 0 582 40621 8 (pbk.)

Printed in Great Britain by Picton Print
Citadel Works, Bath Road, Chippenham, Wilts SN15 2AB

PP41956

CONTENTS

ACKNOWLEDGEMENTS

The original idea for compiling a check-list of football postcards came from a fellow collector, Paul Macnamara, and much of the information incorporated here should be considered a collaborative effort. Peter Grady not only allowed me to extract details of his cards, but invited my plundering his collection for illustration material. Eric Emmett provided a glimpse into the 'Bray' collection, lent cards for inclusion in this book and shared his encyclopaedic knowledge of early football. George Quinn painstakingly photocopied all his football postcards. David Koos generously loaned several cards. Nigel Bishop and Jim Gray provided details of Brighton cards and publishers. Bryan Horsnell gave postcards a welcome mention in his regular feature for *Football Monthly*, and also supplied information from his collection. I wish to express my gratitude to all of the above, but none of them is of course, in any way responsible for resulting inaccuracies or inelegancies of presentation.

Picture Postcards and Their Publishers by Anthony Byatt, and *Association Football and English Society 1863-1915* by Tony Mason have both been invaluable sources of guidance and information.

I would like to thank Veldale and Fisa for readily giving permission to reproduce their postcards.

John Silvester not only designed the cover, but also offered constructive and much-appreciated advice. The staff at Pictons coped with my inscrutable hieroglyphics, and finally to Longman I offer my thanks for their interest in this project.

PREFACE

Today, the picture postcard is an unobtrusive and largely inconsequential fact of life. It was not always so. During the first two decades of this century, Britain was deluged by a flood of these pictorial cards, and it would be no great exaggeration to claim that there were postcards of everything. The term 'Golden Age' has been accorded to these years and the designation accepted as 'official', mainly due to the publication of a seminal book, *Picture Postcards of the Golden Age* by Tonie and Valmai Holt.

Collecting old postcards is now a popular and well-established recreation; some would even say, obsession. Details of publishers, artists, sets and series are emerging piece-meal thanks to the efforts of collectors, enthusiasts and study-groups. It is a truism of 'deltiology' that original trade lists are either non-existent or too sketchy to satisfy, and that knowledge proceeds by examining cards and collating information from various sources.

This book is an attempt to record the assault made by postcard publishers on Association Football at the turn of the century. It was not my original intention to include cards from the 1920s and beyond, but since the story of postcards does not end at 1918, space is also devoted to these 'non-gilded' specimens.

I have tried to illustrate at least one card from most of the important pre-First World War publishers, although the work of the strictly local publisher has of necessity been covered selectively, rather than comprehensively.

These pages should also convince that football is neither totally 'artless' nor humourless, but if the sport occasionally suffers the affliction of taking itself a little too seriously, then a potent antidote resides in a generous overdose of the Edwardian whimsy of Tom Browne or Donald McGill.

Eric Krieger
London 1983

PROLOGUE

Football to 1900 . . .

Football is an ancient sport. Its origins are obscured by the shroud of time, although references are increasingly found in mediaeval, Tudor, Georgian and Victorian writings. Its evolution has spawned several variants: Rugby Union, Rugby League, Australian, American, Gaelic and most pervasive of all, Association or 'Soccer'.

Association Football is a British invention, and one of Britain's most successful exports. By mid-Victorian times the mob-football of the people had been adopted by the public schools, adapted by them to suit their individual playing needs and integrated into an educational philosophy stressing team-spirit, stoicism and general character development.

Students at Cambridge, realising the need to find a universal system of rules to enable players from the various schools to play together, formulated one such scheme in 1848, revised it in 1856 and again in 1863. It was with these latest Cambridge rules in mind that a number of London-based players met together on a Monday evening in October 1863, at the Freemason's Tavern on Great Queen Street, off London's famous Drury Lane. The meeting moved, seconded and duly carried a resolution believing it 'advisable that a football association should be formed for the purpose of settling a code of rules for the regulation of the game of football'. The Football Association thus came into being on the evening of 26 October 1863. It was not until several meetings later that a final draft was agreed, the Association opting for a game in which running with the ball in the hands was forbidden, and 'hacking' disallowed, or else, feared the anti-hackers, 'no one who has arrived at the years of discretion will play at football.'

At first the Association was a grouping of clubs based in or near London, but it quickly acquired affiliates from beyond the capital and as the century advanced, other city and county associations were formed. Many of these still adhered to their own rules in local matches, for example the Sheffield Association, founded in 1867, did not adopt London regulations until ten years later, and indeed played a series of inter-association games against London under 'mixed' rules.

The event that assured the dominance of the London Association was the introduction of a challenge cup in 1871, the brainchild of the then secretary, Charles Alcock. The first final was played on the Kennington Oval before a crowd of 2,000, who saw Alcock's team, the Wanderers, defeat the Royal Engineers by one goal to nil. That year also saw the first official international match, when England and Scotland each failed to score in a drawn game at Partick.

Early Association Football was a game played by gentlemen. It was a sport of honour, if bruising honour, where off-side was 'sneaking' and ungentlemanly

6

conduct was ungentlemanly conduct. By the 1880s the centre of gravity of the game was moving towards the industrial towns and cities of the North and Midlands. In 1883 the spinners and weavers of Blackburn Olympic defeated the Old Etonians in the FA Cup final; two years later the FA acceded to professionalism and in 1889 Preston North End were the first winners of the newly-instituted Football League. During the 1890s football increased in popularity as both a participation and spectator sport, so that by the year 1900 soccer was firmly embedded in the consciousness of the nation.

. . . and Postcards

It was at the turn of the century that football encountered the picture postcard. The Austrian authorities introduced the world's first postcard in October 1869, and one year later the British Post Office issued their first official postcard. These early cards were not pictorial postcards, but plain issues with an imprinted stamp. The introduction of these 'open letters' did not pass without comment, and several correspondents to newspapers feared for the sensibilities of postal delivery workers exposed to these unshielded missives. No notable case of undue mental disequilibrium is recorded.

In 1872 Britain permitted privately printed cards, although these still required an official embossed stamp, but in 1894 the Post Office decided that postcards could be used with a separately affixed postage stamp. It was this concession that gave the go-ahead to the private companies to market their pictorial cards. However, size restrictions still limited design opportunities, and it was not until 1899 that the larger standard-sized cards were accepted.

The Golden Age

The improved scope for postcard designs afforded by the increased size, saw a bewildering range of themes depicted on cards, and a mania sweep the country that did not subside until after the First World War when the postcard rate was doubled. These years have rightly been termed the postcard's 'Golden Age', and it is the attention payed to Association Football by these early postcard publishers, photographers, artists and designers that this book is chiefly concerned.

It was an age when the game was played with an attacking flourish and embellished with individual skill. Players such as Meredith, Bloomer, Woodward and Buchan are still revered; others are consigned to oblivion and the reference books. The Southern League was then still strong, the new Players' Union flexed its muscles and the amateurs of the South seceded from the FA between 1906 and 1914 over the issue of professional registration in their County Associations. This era, beyond two world wars and increasingly beyond memory, is uniquely captured on these unassuming pictorial cards.

GOLDEN AGE PUBLISHERS
THE ACTRESS, THE BISHOP AND
WEST BROMWICH ALBION

The postcard album was one of the clichés of the Edwardian era. The introduction of the larger, standard-sized postcards in 1899 had given an impetus to the postcard mania that swept the country from the turn of the century until the outbreak of war in 1914. There were over 900 million postcards sent in 1914, the vast majority of these, picture postcards. These cards were not only intended to convey messages, but many were acquired to be exchanged, collected, and preserved in decorated albums. The ever increasing demand for these rectangular souvenirs thus witnessed a mushrooming of publishers keen to satisfy this voracious market. Anthony Byatt, in his *Picture Postcards and Their Publishers*, lists several hundred of the leading postcard companies, excluding the local photographers and publishers whose offerings were of only parochial interest. The variety of subjects depicted was as rich as life itself, and in some instances even death, with executions, cemeteries and *in memoriam* cards to be found alongside the trains, trams, politicians, scenic views, seaside piers, Art Nouveau, cats, comic and many, many others. The managing director of the Rotary Photographic Company was quoted in 1906 as claiming, 'there is usually a good sale for preachers, the most popular at present being the Archbishop of Canterbury, the Bishop of London, the Rev R. J. Campbell and Dr Campbell Morgan.' Accompanying the bishop, of course, the actress, and if the numbers of surviving cards are any measure of earlier popularity, then the images of Zena Dare, Billie Burke and Lily Langtry were sought with at least the avidity of the devotees of these reverend gentlemen.

Since the 1880s, soccer had increasingly become the sport of the people. Attendances at the leading venues had increased throughout the 1890s, and by 1900 'five-figure' crowds were commonplace. The late Victorian years had seen the emergence of the football celebrity, and so Association Football was an obvious candidate for inclusion in the themes covered by the early postcard publishers. In this chapter we will detail some of the cards of football players and teams issued by the leading companies before the First World War. Postcards produced by lesser publishers, and local photographers/publishers are discussed in the following chapters. Comic and artistic cards are also dealt with elsewhere.

One of the fascinations of postcard collecting is the vast unknown and uncharted landscape of the subject. In other, long-established collecting fields – eg stamps, coins and cigarette cards – the collectables were produced in a controlled and well-documented manner. Detailed catalogues and check-lists exist to define the boundaries of the quest. Since most of the leading postcard publishers have not bequeathed details of their trade lists, either because such records were not preserved, or have been destroyed by fire or bombing, it has

Celebrated "Association" Football Clubs — NEW BROMPTON 1902—3.

1

GOLDEN AGE PUBLISHERS – FIRST DIVISION

FAMOUS FOOTBALL PLAYERS: — J. W. SUTCLIFFE.

2

Celebrated Football Players: — W. J. FOULKE.

3

9

C. BURGESS

C. W. Faulkner & Co.

4

BULL.

FAULKNER & CO. LONDON, E.C.

5

EVERTON FOOTBALL CLUB, SEASON 1902-3.

C. W. Faulkner & Co.

London, E.C.

6

10

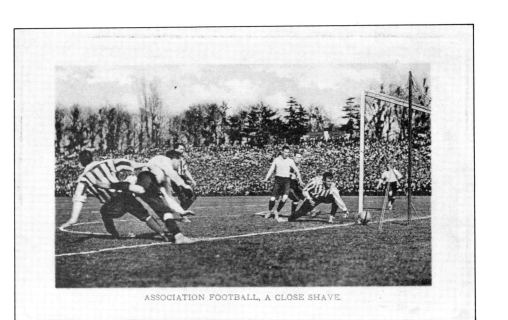

ASSOCIATION FOOTBALL, A CLOSE SHAVE.

7

WILKES.
ASTON VILLA.

8

J. SHARP. EVERTON.

9

No. 333C   **WEST BROMWICH ALBION.**   J. BEAGLES & CO., E.C.

F. EVERISS (Sec.), J. RIFFORD, J. WEBB, R. H. PLAYFAIR, J. PENNINGTON, MR. DEMPSTER,
W. BARBER (Asst. Trainer), A. RANDLE, L. BELL, H. HADLEY, A. LEWIS, J. MANNERS,
W. JUCK, H. BROWN, H. ASTON, G. DORSETT.

10

11

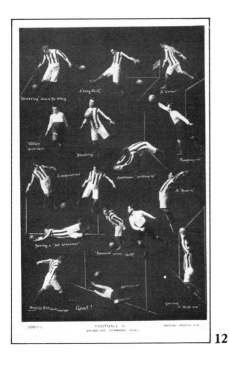

3983 L   FOOTBALL II.   ROTARY PHOTO, E.C.
DRIBBLING, FORWARD, GOAL.

12

A. G. RAISBECK, Liverpool, belongs to Stirlingshire, and is considered one of the best centre-halfs that Scotland has produced. He is a speedy and resourceful player, possessed of excellent judgment. Has represented Scotland in her Association and League Internationals. He is 5 ft. 9½ in. in height, and weighs 12 st. 9 lbs.

13

10513—70   LONDON LIFE.   FOOTBALL. CHELSEA v. ASTON VILLA AT STAMFORD BRIDGE.   ROTARY PHOTO, E.C.
THE IMMENSE CROWDS OF ENTHUSIASTIC FOLLOWERS OF THE GAME RAPIDLY INCREASE WITH EACH SEASON.

14

CHELSEA F.C.
1905

WATSON, McROBERTS, KEY, WINDRIDGE, MACKIE, FOULKE, COPELAND, J.T. ROBERTSON, McEWAN, MORAN, KIRWAN.

NOTTS. FOREST. F.C. 1908-9.

H. HALLAM,   T. GIBSON.   H. WHITCHURCH.   G. NEEDHAM.   G. WOLFE.   W. J. SHEARMAN.   W. DUDLEY.   R. NORRIS.
SEC.   TRAINER.
          W. HOOPER.   T. MARRISON.   E. J. WEST.   A. G. MORRIS.   W. A SPOUNCER.   W. BIRCH.

RAPID PHOTO. E.C.   5142
                          E. HUGHES   G. H. MALTBY   J. ARMSTRONG.
                                         CAPTAIN.

Charlie Roberts.
English International
Centre Half.

17

WILLIAM WEDLOCK
A FAMOUS ENGLISH INTERNATIONAL.

18

Steve Bloomer the King of English Internationals.

19

Harold Fleming
The English International Wizard.

20

HEALTH & STRENGTH SERIES

QUEEN'S PARK RANGERS F.C.

21

OXO for Stamina.

PORTSMOUTH F.C. 1904-5
Photo by STEPHEN CRIBB, Southsea.

22

KEY TO ILLUSTRATIONS PAGES 9 TO 16

1 Raphael Tuck & Sons' series 940 – Celebrated Association Football Clubs – 'New Brompton 1902–3'. Known today as Gillingham FC, these Kentish men played under the earlier moniker until 1913.

2 Raphael Tuck & Sons' series 900 – Famous Football Players – 'J.W.Sutcliffe'. Sutcliffe played international football for England in both the association and rugby codes. This series of six cards also includes the Corinthian centre-forward G. O. Smith, and all-round sportsman C. B. Fry.

3 Raphael Tuck & Sons' series 899 – Celebrated Football Players – 'W. J. Foulke'. Larger than life in more ways than one, this former Sheffield United and Chelsea custodian later became an attraction on Blackpool's Golden Mile. Foulke weighed over 20 stones in his Chelsea days, although this postcard of c1902–3 is based on a photograph of the mid-1890s and shows a youthful and slimline pose.

4 C. W. Faulkner & Co – 'C. Burgess'.

5 C. W. Faulkner & Co – 'Bull'. Posted in April 1903, we see Walter Bull during his Notts County time. He later played for Spurs, and was a team-mate there of Herbert Chapman. It was Walter Bull, who, declining the offer of manager's post at Northampton Town, advised Chapman to apply. Chapman joined Northampton in 1907 as player-manager, before moving on to Leeds City, Huddersfield Town, Arsenal and deification.

6 C. W. Faulkner & Co – 'Everton Football Club, Season 1902–3'.

7 The Wrench series, No. 3838 – Association Football. 'A Close Shave'. Posted in 1904, this goal-mouth incident is from the FA Cup final between Tottenham and Sheffield United three years earlier.

8 The Wrench series, No. 2951 – 'H. Wilkes, Aston Villa'. This autographed card of Albert Wilkes (who corrected the initial as well!) was posted to him by Reginald Bray in November 1903. Bray was the self-styled 'Autograph King', dispatching postcards of well-known celebrities to them for signing and return. This Wrench series of footballers netted him many signatures. Wilkes was a photographer as well as footballer and produced many football postcards himself.

9 The Wrench series, No. 2166 – 'J. Sharp, Everton'. Cricketer and footballer, playing both games for England, and later, director of Everton.

10 The Wrench series, No. 5538 – 'Sunderland Association Football Club 1902–1903'.

11 J. Beagles and Co, No. 333C – 'West Bromwich Albion'. c1905.

12 Rotary Photo, No. 3983L – 'Football II. Dribbling, Forward, Goal'.

13 W. Collins, Sons & Co Ltd – 'Herriot' series – 'A. G. Raisbeck, Liverpool'. From a series of coloured, stylised impressions of English and Scottish international players. Raisbeck made quite a spectacle of himself, being one of the very few players of his standard to wear glasses whilst playing.

14 Rotary Photo, No. 10513-70 – London Life. 'Chelsea v Aston Villa at Stamford Bridge'. A rare card from a much collected series.

15 Rapid Photo Co, No. 2719 – 'Chelsea FC 1905–6'. Chelsea's first season, in which

the Southern League refused their application but the Football League did not. The goalkeeper Foulke is seen modelling big-tops for Barnum and Bailey.

16 Rapid Photo Co, No. 5142 – 'Notts. Forest FC 1908–9'.

17 'Charlie Roberts'.

18 'William Wedlock'.

19 'Steve Bloomer'.

20 'Harold Fleming'. Four cards from a series of twelve by an uncredited publisher. Roberts and Wedlock were rivals for the England centre-half shirt, although Roberts' shirt would, no doubt, have dwarfed the diminutive Wedlock. Roberts was a thorn in the side of the footballing establishment, and possibly because of this, won too little international recognition. Harold Fleming was the pride of Swindon as well being a lay-preacher, and Steve Bloomer was simply Steve Bloomer. The series dates from *c*1912.

21 *Health & Strength* series – 'Queen's Park Rangers FC'. Issued in 1911 by the publishers of this journal of the body beautiful, with teams from England, Scotland, Ireland and Wales.

22 Oxo – 'Portsmouth FC 1904–5'. The secret of Pompey's beefiness revealed.

fallen to collectors to attempt a little postcard archaeology. Football postcards have fortunately yielded many of their secrets, although some mysteries still remain.

If, in 1905, you had asked the man on the Clapham tram to name three postcard publishers, then it is a fair bet that the first name on his lips would have been **Raphael Tuck & Sons.** This company produced an immense number of postcard series, and at present, several study-groups are attempting to reconstruct details of their output, and unravel the complexities of a labyrinthine numbering system. Like so many of the early publishers, their building, Raphael House, was located in the City of London. The premises were bombed in late 1940, destroying all records.

Tuck produced three series of postcards featuring football teams and players. Series number 940, 'Celebrated Association Football Clubs', features six teams from the season 1902-3. They had clearly attempted to appeal to the four corners (and centre) of England with their choice of clubs. From the Midlands were selected Small Heath (who changed their name to Birmingham in 1905), and Aston Villa. Villa were the giants of the 1890s, winning the Football League Championship four years out of five between 1896 and 1900. The choice from the North-East was Newcastle United, who were to become the aristocrats of the Edwardian age. Newcastle were one of the finest teams of any era, with their wealth of Scottish international talent, and delicate close-passing football. Tuck's representative from the South-West seems curious, ignoring the claims of Tottenham and Woolwich Arsenal, in favour of New Brompton, who have been known as Gillingham FC since 1913. The other teams in this series are Everton and Bristol City. Series 899, 'Celebrated Football Players', is a set of six English international stars. Chadwick was of Portsmouth, Molyneux and Robinson were both of Southampton. The Saints were in the football limelight in 1902, having reached the FA Cup final, only to be defeated by Sheffield United. The other players in this set are: Foulke, then of Sheffield United and portrayed as a sylph-like youth, although later he was to expand to exceed 20 stones; Devey of Aston Villa; and John Cox, the Liverpool outside-left. A similar series, 900, 'Famous Football Players', stars the Tottenham goalkeeper, George Clawley, along with the Corinthian immortals, C. B. Fry and G. O. Smith. Also included are Athersmith (Small Heath), Crabtree (Aston Villa), and the international soccer and rugby celebrity, John Sutcliffe. In this series, Sutcliffe is affiliated with Millwall, with whom he stayed from April 1902 until May 1903, and so the date of issue of this set is given approximately.

The founding father of the company of **E. Wrench Ltd,** was John Evelyn Wrench. It was while he was touring in Germany that Wrench decided his fortune was to be made in postcards. Unfortunately his ambitions were not matched by his financial judgement. Cash-flow problems put the company, which ceased trading in 1906, beyond recovery. The cards published by Wrench, each carry individual serial numbers, and it is therefore possible to gauge the span, although the complete details are not yet available.

One series of players with confirmed numbers from 2159 to 2193 was published in 1903, and consists of head-and-shoulder collotype portraits on cards with raised borders. The most represented club in this sequence is Sheffield United, who had appeared in the FA Cup finals of 1901 and 1902. Sheffield could indeed claim to be the soccer-city of the country at this time, with Wednesday winning the League Championship in 1903 and 1904. The Blades included in the set are: Foulke (2174), Thickett (2175), Bennett (2176), Needham (2177), Lipsham (2178), Hedley (2179), Johnson (2184), Barnes (2185), Morren (2186), Priest (2187) and Wilkinson (2188). Several southern players appear in the series, including from Tottenham: Jones (2170), Hughes (2171), Clawley (2172), Kirwin (2182) and Erentz (2183). From Southampton are: Robinson (2159), Molyneux (2161) and Fry (2162) – who also feature in the Tuck series – Wood (2163) and Turner (2191). Along the Hampshire coast at Portsmouth were to be found: Chadwick (2160), Smith (2169), and Brown (2173). John Sharp (2166), Everton's English international outside-right, also played cricket for Lancashire and England. Derby County's goal-shooting superstar Steve Bloomer (2193) carries the flag for the Midlands. A different sequence of cards, also published in 1903, hosts Bloomer's team-mates at Derby: Fryer (2946), Methven (2947) and May (2948), along with the Aston Villa players – George (2949), Garraty (2950) and Wilkes (2951). Derby were the FA Cup finalists in 1903, on the wrong end of a six-goal beating against Bury. Albert Wilkes was a professional photographer and international footballer; and as well as being the subject of postcards, was the originator of many.

One keen purchaser of these Wrench portraits, was Reginald Bray, the self-styled 'Autograph King'. Bray posted cards to well-known personalities, requesting their return complete with signature. At least thirty of the Wrench football series were thus returned, although John Sharp was not so obliging as the others, returning the card unsigned.

Wrench do not appear to have produced many standard group portraits of teams, although a card exists of Sunderland (5538), showing the team of 1902-3. Some action views of the 1901 FA Cup final were sold, bearing the titles 'Association Football, A Slip' (3836), 'Association Football, A Close Shave' (3838), and the oddly captioned, 'Association Football, A Throw Up' (3837). These three cards, seem to have been issued belatedly in 1904. The most attractive set of football cards from Wrench is their c1905 'Famous Football Teams' series. The names of the teams are spelled out in large letters, illuminated with head-and-shoulder portraits of the players. Clubs noted are: Bolton Wanderers (10707), Woolwich Arsenal (10708), Queen's Park Rangers (10709), West Bromwich Albion (10710), Aston Villa (10711), Portsmouth (10712), Sheffield Wednesday (10713), Notts County (10714), Everton (10716) and Tottenham Hotspur (10717).

Both Raphael Tuck and Wrench were marketing collotype portraits of footballers during the first four years of the century. Another early publisher producing similar material was the firm of **C. W. Faulkner & Co Ltd.** Charles Faulkner was a Yorkshireman who studied fine art in France, and later established himself as a colour printer in London. The Faulkner cards have no serial numbers, nor do they even carry a series title. Several cards of Southampton players were published, including Fry, Robinson, Turner, Wood and Molyneux. These players may possibly have been part of a set to commemorate that club's FA Cup final appearance in 1902. Other cards showing the Notts County players, Iremonger and Bull, were issued, as were portraits of Portsmouth's Cunliffe and Burgess. Walter Bull later moved to Tottenham where he was a team-mate of Herbert Chapman. It was only after Bull had rejected the opportunity to become manager at Northampton, that Chapman accepted the post on Bull's advice, and so took a first step to immortality. Team line-ups do not seem to have proved popular with Faulkner, although a group of the 1902–3 Everton side was issued.

It cannot be claimed with any certainty when the first picture postcards featuring leading players and teams appeared, but one can be fairly confident that the companies of Tuck, Wrench and Faulkner were among the first of the major publishers to issue cards of this genre. These three firms produced similar collotype printed cards, sometimes even based on the same original photographs.

Another trio of companies marketing similar products were the Rotary Photographic Company, the Rapid Photo Printing Company and John Beagles & Company. Their cards were largely real-photographic as distinct from gravure, collotype, and half-tone printed. We have already encountered the **Rotary Photographic Company** with its saleable preachers. Also sold in numbers were stage actresses and royalty. Byatt claims that by 1904, this firm was producing a quarter of a million cards per month. It was this year that a series of football team line-ups appeared, numbered as follows: Tottenham Hotspur (3841A), Bolton Wanderers (3842A), West Bromwich Albion (3843A), Preston North End (3844A) and Woolwich Arsenal (3845A). 'Mr George Robey's Football Team' is tagged on at number 3847A. A series of cards illustrating skills from various sports includes two of soccer, 'Football I Passing, Goal & Volley' (3983K), and 'Football II Dribbling, Forward, Goal' (3983L).

John Beagles & Company were also renowned for their output of photographic cards of royalty, actresses and other noteworthy personages. One series of soccer clubs, shows teams for the 1905–6 season. Beagles' numbering system involved a series number followed by a suffix letter identifying the individual card. The '333' series of football teams appears to consist of two sections. The earlier cards are found in a matt bromide finish, the later ones in a glossy format, bearing the prefix 'G'. Most of the teams are from the Football League, although Tottenham Hotspur (333B) of the Southern League was proving popular with postcard publishers. Liverpool (333K) were bouncing back in no uncertain manner; having been relegated in 1904, they won the Second Division title in 1905, and the following season were Football League Champions. Preston North End (333A) and West Bromwich Albion (333C), the two Titans of the 1880s, were featured along with Stoke (333E), Leeds City (333G) and Blackpool (333H). The glossy touch was applied to Blackburn Rovers (G333O), and Wolverhampton Wanderers (G333P).

Producers of postcards depicting football teams and individual players, as distinct from humorous and artistic designs, fall into two broad categories. There were the large, and perhaps, not so large companies, issuing a range of cards intended to have a geographically extensive market. These are the publishers dealt with in this section of the book. The other class of producers, were locally based. Very often they were photographers, selling photographs in postcard format, to a parochial clientele. This latter group, in many cases, would photograph the team and players each season, and so it is possible to acquire a collection of cards following one club through successive years. The other group of publishers, such as Tuck, Beagles, Faulkner, etc, usually produced just one or two sequences of these cards, and then never again.

One of the notable exceptions were the **Rapid Photo Printing Company**. This firm published photographic postcards for about nine years from 1901. Although we do not have full details of their football postcards, what is clear is that from the season 1904–5, until 1908–9, they issued one series of cards each year. The company ceased trading around 1910, and so the cut-off year is explained.

The first cards produced were matt prints and teams recorded so far include Preston North End (1727), Sheffield Wednesday (1801) and the newly-promoted Woolwich Arsenal (1726). The cards for the following season, 1905–6, and subsequent years were glossy photographic prints. Chelsea's dramatic elevation to League status in 1905 is captured in a team line-up in the goal mouth at Stamford Bridge. This card (2719), showing the first-ever Chelsea team, is dominated by their newly-acquired goalkeeper, Foulke, who was by this time approaching the dimensions of a barrage balloon. The caption to the Birmingham (2764) team group, reminds purchasers that the club was 'Late Small Heath'. The club changed its title that year, in the hope of gaining a stronger local identity, and with it some success, but the record books show that it was still Aston Villa's (2686) city. Other teams issued in 1905–6 were: Notts Forest (2716), Notts County (2717), Tottenham Hotspur (2720), Stoke (2721), Liverpool (2722).

The cards produced by the Rapid Company were of teams mostly from the North and Midlands, although the Bristol City (4830) group of 1907–8 is sandwiched between Bury (4829) and West Bromwich Albion (4831). The season 1906–7 included: Blackburn Rovers (4342), Stoke (4345) and West Bromwich Albion (4347). Their final year of production, 1908–9, offered: Bradford City (5145), Blackburn Rovers (5146), Bury (5147), Notts County (5148), Manchester City (5152), with Queen's Park Rangers (5314) trailing along.

No account of the leading postcard publishers would be complete without some mention of the Dundee firm of **Valentine & Sons**. From the last century to well after the Second World War, the Scottish factories of this company produced postcards by the million. Valentine produced several humorous postcards taking a whimsical look at football, and further mention will be made in a later chapter. They also issued a series of leading football players in the early 1950s, at a time when other publishers had long since ignored soccer. However, one of their most sought after series of football-related cards was issued c1905.

A set of vertical, coloured souvenir designs of leading English clubs was created, each showing an artist-drawn player in team colours, with the name of the club and the ground. Teams on offer included: Aston Villa, Notts Forest, Sheffield Wednesday and Sunderland. A similar series was also issued at roughly the same time, under the general title, 'The Scottish Teams Series'. The reputation of this company was made in its extensive range of local view cards, and it is doubtful whether a single hamlet escaped their attentions. A view of the 'Aston Villa Football Ground, Birmingham', in 1905, would have been included in these topographical lists, rather than the sporting.

During the Golden Age of the picture postcard, hundreds of card publishers flourished in Britain. They ranged from the one-man business in the local high street, selling a small selection of local scenic views, to the giant printing companies with their rotary presses and legions of technicians, artists, photographers and salesmen. The companies discussed in this chapter were in the First Division of publishers. Some may have been active for only a few years, whilst others traded for decades, but what they shared in common was the vast quantity and timeless quality of their products.

GOLDEN AGE PUBLISHERS - SECOND DIVISION

The journal *Health & Strength,* was established in 1898, and only eight years later was already claiming to be 'the oldest and most widely circulating Physical Culture Magazine in the world'. Although 'under no circumstances [were] advertisements of Alchoholic Liquors, Patent Medicines or Tobacco' to be inserted, readers were invited to write for details of the 'Clease-Extensor' method of height increase. This 'Rational and Scientific System' would increase the height from 1 to 2½ inches with added 'Strength, Health and Bodily Beauty'. For those whose bodily beauty was leading to the path of temptation, Doctor Sylvanus Stall's books in 'The Self & Sex' series, offered cautionary guidance. The September 1906 edition provided articles on 'Wrestling in India', and the Kentish Samson, Richard Joy, who, at the commencement of the eighteenth century lifted a weight of 2,240 lb, broke a rope capable of supporting 35 cwts and pulled successfully against a horse of 'unusual power'. His aquatic prowess proved, however, fatally inadequate, as he drowned in 1742. The main feature though, in this particular edition, on the eve of the coming 1906–7 football season, was the 'opinions of internationals on training and diet'.

The cover portrayed the Newcastle United half-back, Colin Veitch, who, the magazine claimed, was arguably 'the best all-round footballer in England at the present time'. Not for the Corinthian G. O. Smith, we read, the vigorous exercises and abstemious life, claiming never actually to train, and that a game of fives or racquets every day should prove quite sufficient. Sheffield's Ernest Needham advised athletes to 'shun spirits as if they were poison', Johnny Goodall, the former Preston and Derby County international, limiting himself to a 'lemon and a dash'.

Association football was honoured again by the attentions of the *Health & Strength* magazine in 1911, when they produced a series of postcards of leading English, Irish and Scottish teams. The Welsh were acknowledged through the Cardiff and Swansea rugby fifteens. The frequency with which early postcards now appear in dealers' stocks is a good indication of the numbers in which they were originally issued. The *Health & Strength* series is one of the most frequently recurring sets, and so we can conclude that they were sold in fair quantity. Scotland's representative in the series is Glasgow Rangers, and from Ireland we find Shelbourne FC. The English clubs include two from the North and two from the South, with the Midlands seemingly excluded. Queen's Park Rangers and Swindon Town carry the southern flag. Swindon were the Southern League Champions in the season 1910–11, and so their inclusion is understandable, as is the choice of Manchester United, the Football League Champions in the same season. These two teams met later in an amazing Charity Shield match in 1912, United winning by eight goals to four. This pre-First World War Manchester United team was one of their finest ever, with Meredith, Charlie Roberts, George Wall and Bell playing in a multi-talented

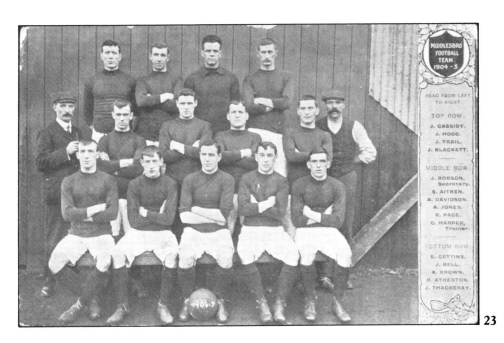

23

GOLDEN AGE PUBLISHERS - SECOND DIVISION

W.E.HEMINGFIELD.   J. STEWART.   T.L JARVIS.   W BARTLETT.
J. DAVIS.   R. FERRIER.   A. LANGLEY   J LYALL   T.GRAWSHAW   W LAYTON   H. BURTON.   H. RUDDLESDEN   P.FRITH.

24

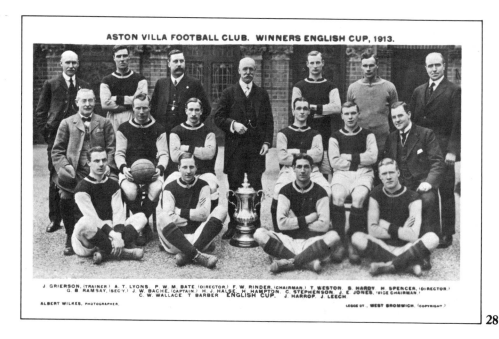

ASTON VILLA FOOTBALL CLUB. WINNERS ENGLISH CUP, 1913.

J. GRIERSON, (TRAINER) A. T. LYONS. P. W. M. BATE (DIRECTOR.) F. W. RINDER. (CHAIRMAN.) T. WESTON. S. HARDY. H. SPENCER. (DIRECTOR.)
G. B. RAMSAY, (SEC'Y.) J. W. BACHE, (CAPTAIN.) H. J. HALSE. H. HAMPTON. C. STEPHENSON. J. E. JONES. (VICE CHAIRMAN.)
C. W. WALLACE. T. BARBER. ENGLISH CUP. J. HARROP. J. LEECH.

ALBERT WILKES, PHOTOGRAPHER.

LEGGE ST., WEST BROMWICH. (COPYRIGHT.)

28

NEWCASTLE UNITED F.C.
ENGLISH CUP TEAM.

A.AITKEN W.McCRACKEN A.GOSNELL J.HOWIE
A.McCOMBIE P.McWILLIAM J.RUTHERFORD R.ORR
J.LAWRENCE J.CARR G.VEITCH

THE CRYSTAL PALACE GROUND.

29

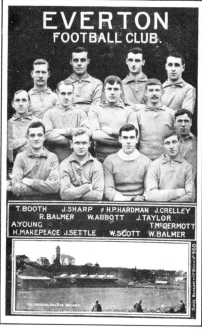

EVERTON
FOOTBALL CLUB.

T.BOOTH J.SHARP H.P.HARDMAN J.CRELLEY
R.BALMER W.ABBOTT J.TAYLOR
A.YOUNG T.McDERMOTT
H.MAKEPEACE J.SETTLE W.SCOTT W.BALMER

THE CRYSTAL PALACE GROUND.

30

27

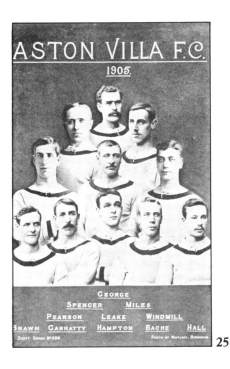

ASTON VILLA F.C.
1905.

GEORGE
SPENCER   MILES
PEARSON   LEAKE   WINDMILL
BRAWN GARRATTY HAMPTON BACHE   HALL

SCOTT SERIES №484

PHOTO BY WHITLOCK, BIRMINGHAM

25

SMALL HEATH F.C.
1905.

ROBINSON
GLOVER   STOKES
BEER   WIGMORE   DOUGHERTY
TICKLE   GREEN   JONES   WILCOX   FIELD

SCOTT SERIES №493

PHOTO BY WHITLOCK, BIRMINGHAM

26

Manchester United F.C. 1st League Champions 1910-11.
Team for Season 1911-12.

27

CORINTHIANS F. C.

Harrower (Referee)   K. R. G. Hunt   G. S. Harris   T. S. Rowlandson   C. C. Page   F. D. Craig   R. D. Craig   H. W. Hewitt (Linesman)
W. U. Timmis   S. H. Day   S. S. Harris   G. C. Vassall   C. G. D. Wright

31

NORTHERN NOMADS TEAM.

J. P. McKenna, R. T. Wallwork, L. R. Roose, H. Thomas, "Barney" Browne, T. H. Jackson,
Hon. Sec.
H. P. Hardman, S. B. Ashworth, F. Walmsley, V. S. Simpson, E. Mansfield, R. Stephenson.

32

ENGLISH INTERNATIONAL TEAM.

Pennington   Williamson   Crompton
K. R. G. Hunt   Wedlock   Warren
Evans   V. Woodward   G. W. Webb   Fleming   Simpson

33

WALES.

C. Morris   L. R. Roose   Hewitt
Hughes   Lloyd Davies   Llew Davies
Vizard   A. G. Morris   W. Davies   Evan Jones   W. Meredith

34

OLDHAM ATHLETIC A.F.C.

Matthews
Cook   Hodson
Wilson   Walders   Moffatt
Donnachie   Woodger   Jones   Montgomery   Broad

35

NEWCASTLE UNITED A.F.C.

Whitson   McCracken
McWilliam   Lawrence   Veitch
Wilson   Higgins   Low   Higdon   Stewart   Rutherford

36

Photo by R. Scott & Co., Manchester. **BRISTOL CITY (Cup Team).**

Hardy   Marr

Mr. H. Thickett, Man   Mr F. W. Bacon, Dir. Annan Young Clay Cottle Rippon Batten, Tra.

Spear Staniforth Gilligan Maxwell Burton Hilton Wedlock Hanlin

Photo by R. Scott & Co., Manchester. **MANCHESTER UNITED (Cup Team).**

F. Bacon, Tra.   H. Halse W. Meredith H. Moger J. Picken G. Wall Stacey H. Burgess

A. Turnbull   J. Turnbull   R. Duckworth C. Roberts, Capt. A. Bell V. Hayes Mr. Mangnall, Sec.

G. Livingstone   A. Downie

INTERNATIONAL.
Souvenir.

ENGLAND.

SCOTLAND.

WALES.

IRELAND.

ASSOCIATION.

39

R. E. EVANS, Sheffield United.
English International.
Has also played for Wales.

1911   versus Scotland.
1911-12   ..   Wales.
1911   ..   Ireland.

40

Football Celebrities.

Hope they will win
the cup next year

W. GEORGE (Aston Villa).

41

31

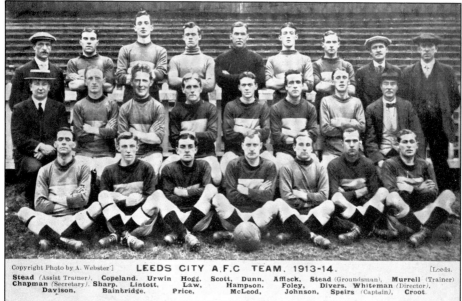

Copyright Photo by A. Webster] **LEEDS CITY A.F.C TEAM, 1913-14.** [Leeds.

Stead (Assist Trainer), **Copeland, Urwin Hogg, Scott, Dunn, Affleck, Stead** (Groundsman), **Murrell** (Trainer)
Chapman (Secretary), **Sharp, Lintott, Law, Hampson, Foley, Divers, Whiteman** (Director),
Davison, Bainbridge, Price, McLeod, Johnson, Speirs (Captain), **Croot.**

42

West Ham F.C. 1910-11

43

32

KEY TO ILLUSTRATIONS PAGES 25 TO 32

23 Delittle, Fenwick & Co Ltd, 'D.F. & Co' series – 'Middlesbro' Football Team 1904-5'.

24 Delittle, Fenwick & Co Ltd, 'D.F. & Co' series – 'Sheffield Wednesday League Team 1904-5'. Other teams featured in this series include Liverpool, Everton, Newcastle United and Wolverhampton Wanderers.

25 Scott Russell & Co, 'Scott' series, No.484 – 'Aston Villa FC 1905'. Villa won the FA Cup this year, and the card was re-issued, overprinted with 'Winners English Cup'.

26 Scott Russell & Co, 'Scott' series, No.495 – 'Small Heath FC 1905'. Small Heath certainly did not win the FA Cup in 1905, and changing their title to Birmingham FC that year, still left them living in the shadow of their successful neighbours. Both of these Scott Russell cards are posed in a popular Edwardian triangular formation; goalkeeper at the apex, forwards providing the base, with the full-backs and half-backs between.

27 Albert Wilkes – 'Manchester United FC. 1st League Champions 1910-11. Team for Season 1911-12'. A card from the camera of Albert Wilkes, who had given up football in 1909 following a fire at his studio, to devote himself completely to sports photography. He proceeded to record most leading football teams and players throughout the 1920s, continuing until his death in 1936. His son carried on with the business until the 1960s.

28 Albert Wilkes – 'Aston Villa Football Club. Winners English Cup, 1913'. Villa defeated Sunderland in the final, before 120,000 people at the Crystal Palace, but were runners-up to them in the League Championship. Wilkes played for Aston Villa before his transfer to Fulham in 1907.

29 Scott Russell & Co, 'Scott' series, No.957 – 'Newcastle United FC. English Cup Team'.

30 Scott Russell & Co, 'Scott' series, No.960 – 'Everton Football Club'. Two souvenirs of the 1906 FA Cup final from Scott Russell. Newcastle lost the final for the second year running.

31 R. Scott & Co, Manchester – 'Corinthians FC'. The 1880s and 1890s had seen the best Corinthian teams, but in the early 1900s they were still able to compete with the leading professional sides. They defeated the 1903 FA Cup holders, Bury, by 10 goals to 3! This team of 1906 includes the Rev K. R. G. Hunt, Muscular Christianity writ large, who played for England, and won an FA Cup winner's medal with the Wolves in 1908.

32 R. Scott & Co, Manchester – 'Northern Nomads Team'. The Nomads embraced the same amateur ideals as the Corinthians. The team shown here of 1907 includes H. P. Hardman who won an FA Cup winner's medal with Everton in 1906, and was Manchester United chairman at the time of the Munich air disaster.

33 R. Scott & Co, Manchester – 'English International Team'.

34 R. Scott & Co, Manchester – 'Wales'.

35 R. Scott & Co, Manchester – 'Oldham Athletic AFC'.

36 R. Scott & Co, Manchester – 'Newcastle United AFC'. Four cards from a series of international and club sides c1911–12.

37 R. Scott & Co, Manchester – 'Bristol City (Cup Team)'.

38 R. Scott & Co, Manchester – 'Manchester United (Cup Team)'. The two 1909 FA Cup finalists, Turnbull for United, shooting the only goal. He was later banned for life, following a bribery scandal.

39 R. Scott & Co, Manchester – 'International Souvenir'. Home international teams 1905.

40 'R. E. Evans, Sheffield United'. Uncredited publisher. From a series of similar studies, possibly six in number. It was not at first realised that Evans was eligible to play for England, having previously played for Wales. In 1911 however, he exchanged the red shirt for the white, as this card testifies.

41 Birmingham Novelty Co, Art Publishers, 'Football' series – 'Football Celebrities. W. George (Aston Villa)'. This series of coloured head-and-shoulder studies was issued c1905, and features players from Aston Villa, Small Heath and West Bromwich Albion. The card was posted shortly after Villa had returned with the 'Tin God' in 1905. 'Hope they will win the cup next year', reads the message from Gert, but the FA Cup was never any respecter of hopes, Everton taking the trophy in 1906.

42 Joe Booth, Leeds – 'Leeds City AFC Team 1913–14'. Herbert Chapman in his second managerial rôle. Joe Booth published several similar cards of northern teams between 1910 and 1914.

43 London *Evening Times* – 'West Ham United' (1908–9, not 1910–11 as inked in). Issued in connection with a competion with £150 first prize for a correct prediction of the Cup Final score.

star-studded line-up. The sixth soccer team in this set of postcards is Bradford City. In 1911, as everyone knows in that Woollen Capital, Bradford City won the FA Cup, beating Newcastle, in a replayed game at the recently-opened Old Trafford. This *Health & Strength* card shows the proud team with the gleaming new trophy, the first club to win the present cup, the previous pot having been donated to Lord Kinnaird. The prize was, curiously enough, fashioned by a Bradford firm of silversmiths.

The publishers of the *Health & Strength* magazine would not have been considered main-stream postcard producers and neither would the Glasgow book publishers **William Collins & Sons**. This company is still producing its dictionaries and Bibles, but in 1903 they started to issue sets of picture post-cards. The cards are identified as the 'Herriot Series', from the location of the company's Glasgow premises in Herriot Hill. As well as publishing a number of humorous football studies, this firm also issued packets of stylised artists' impressions of leading Scottish and English international players. These highly collectable cards are brightly coloured and carry brief biographical details in 'pen-pictures' at the bottom of the obverse side. At least three sets of six were printed, and sold in envelopes carrying the title, 'Famous Footballers'. The players represented in these sets include Baddeley of Wolverhampton Wanderers, and another celebrated goalkeeper, Doig of Sunderland. The Corinthian spirit was represented by that prince of centre-forwards, G. O. Smith, and the all-round athlete C. B. Fry. The Liverpool centre-half, Rais-beck, is described on the card as 'speedy and resourceful ... possessed of excellent judgment'. It does not mention that he was one of the few players of international standard, to actually play matches wearing spectacles. As well as by Doig, Sunderland's name is carried by McCombie and Watson. Their neighbours, Newcastle, claimed R. S. McColl, the Glasgow-born centre-forward. The Sheffield United giant, W. Foulke and Bury's John Plant hailed from the North of England; with Crabtree of Aston Villa from the Midlands. The Lancashire-born Arthur Chadwick played his most successful football on the southern coast with Southampton and Portsmouth, as did fellow Lan-castrian, Albert Houlker.

W. H. Smith & Son issued their cards under different series headings, one of which was the 'Kingsway Series'. Many of the cards in this series were of real photographic views, the cards carrying individual serial numbers. There has been no identified large-scale football output as such, but a couple of cards have been recorded, 'Association Football Cup Final Crystal Palace' (S6336), and 'Association Football Cup Final Crowd Crystal Palace' (S6335). The latter card shows a section of the enormous crowd which gathered for the 1901 FA Cup final between Tottenham and Sheffield United. This was the first 'six-figure' gate, and perhaps noteworthy enough to preserve on a postcard, although the card was not actually produced until round about 1910. The other view is of a panoramic glimpse of the match in progress in 1909, when Manchester United defeated Bristol City by Turnbull's goal.

The initials D. F. & Co., betray the firm of **Delittle, Fenwick & Company** of York. Founded in 1903, this publisher offered a wide range of postcard themes including, for the season 1904–5, a set of popular football teams from the North and Midlands. Each card shows the players, with their names identified at the bottom of the picture, and the club name, along with 1904–5, inside a small shield. Sheffield Wednesday, the League Champions for the previous two seasons, are included along with Newcastle United, who were to become champions in 1904–5, as well as losing FA Cup finalists. During the 1904–5 struggles, Middlesbrough felt the need to pay a record £1,000 to secure the transfer of Alf Common from Sunderland and thereby astonish the football world. Middlesbrough probably thought their money well invested, as First Division status was preserved after looking possible relegation fodder. Common was not, however, signed in time to line-up with his new colleagues for the postcard photograph. Two teams in the set that were to enjoy contrasting fortunes during the following season, were Liverpool and Wolverhampton Wanderers. Whilst Liverpool won the First Division title, Wolves managed to finish bottom of the table in 1906. These were without doubt halcyon times for Everton, who ended the 1904–5 season runners-up to Newcastle in the League, and overcame the same side at the Crystal Palace the following year to win the FA Cup. They were also finalists in the 1907 FA Cup competition, but the Sheffield Owls proved their masters.

To many people, the initials 'B.B.' evoke memories of the Boys' Brigade, with its church-parade, off-key bugles and pill-box hats, whilst others may conjure up images of a pouting French celluloid dream, but to any self-respecting deltiologist, they mean one thing only. The company of **Birn Brothers Ltd**, was producing Fine Art goods before the turn of the century. After 1900 they started to produce picture postcards. One series of their cards is familiar to anyone who has ever tackled a dealer's 'Sport' box in the search for football gems. Series E41, issued before 1910, and on sale for several years before the Great War, freezes several moments of soccer action. Each card is hand-tinted in a 'wooden' frame and based on a photograph of football incidents from the grounds of prominent clubs, or in the case of the card captioned, 'Well Saved', from the old Crystal Palace. The teams involved and the venues chosen, are not identified, although it is possible to recognise the card, 'A Throw In From Touch Line', as Villa Park in Birmingham. The remaining captions are: 'A Neat Dribble', 'An Anxious Moment', 'A Back Clearing' and 'A Run By The Forwards'. A far more difficult series to trap, is the G11 set of football teams. This series of coloured team groups was issued a little before the E41 sequence and includes: Stoke, Notts County, Bristol City and Preston North End.

The Fulham match programme, in January 1908, advised its readers that the team photograph postcard could be obtained on the ground, price one (pre-decimal) penny. It was, they opined 'well worth the humble brown charged for it'. This same journal, at the beginning of the 1907–8 season, their first in the Football League, described one of their new signings as 'Wilkes, A; from Walsall Swifts and Aston Villa. Has had five English caps as a right half. Needless to say, he is a delightful player to watch'. This 'delightful Wilkes, A.' was the photographer responsible for the above-mentioned team postcard.

Albert Wilkes had served an apprenticeship in the late 1890s with the Wolverhampton photographer, G. O. Guggenheim. Wilkes' football talents had interested the most successful club of the era, Aston Villa, who signed him in 1898 from Walsall Swifts. It was at Villa Park that his play earned him international recognition, playing five times for England, including the tragic 1902 game at Ibrox stadium in Glasgow when twenty-six people were killed following the collapse of a section of the ground. The most influential football journalist of the time was James Catton, editor of *Athletic News*, and it was Catton who advised Albert Wilkes to combine his photographic training and knowledge of football, by specialising in sports photography.

Setting up a studio in Legge Street, West Bromwich, he proceeded to photograph the leading teams and star players of his time. Wilkes' tenure at Fulham was short-lived and in the Spring of 1909 he moved to Chesterfield Town. His active playing career in Derbyshire was to last only a few weeks, for in the close-season, a fire gutted his studio, causing not only structural damage, but destroying irreplacable plates and negatives. Wilkes promptly decided to retire from football and rebuild his business. From this time, up until his death in 1936, he continued to photograph prominent club and representative teams. Many were issued as postcards and although he would not have thought of himself as a specialist postcard publisher, but rather as a general sports photographer, he should not go unmentioned in the context of this book. It is not possible to list all the cards produced by Wilkes, although his beloved Aston Villa, with whom he took a directorship in 1934, feature prominently. Many cards were of teams visiting the nearby West Bromwich Albion ground and he also produced team photographs of the 1914 FA Cup finalists, Burnley and Liverpool. Following his father's death, Wilkes' son, Albert Junior, continued with the business until the 1960s. The Wilkes' collection was later acquired by the specialist picture agency, *Colorsport*, in North London and now forms the basis of their early football archive.

The establishing of a challenge cup competition in 1871 was the key event that consolidated the dominance of the London Football Association. The first final was played on 16 March 1872, at the Surrey County Cricket ground at the Kennington Oval. The Wanderers team that defeated the Royal Engineers, included the FA Secretary, C. W. Alcock, whose brainchild, the competition was. A crowd of only 2,000 assembled to witness the historic event. Nearly thirty years later, in 1901, over 100,000 people converged on the Crystal Palace grounds at Sydenham, to see Tottenham and Sheffield United play out a drawn game. From 1895 until 1914, this South London venue was the focal point of the year for thousands of working-class men from the industrial centres in the North and Midlands. Despite the occasional interlopers, such as Southampton in 1900 and 1902, Spurs as mentioned in 1901 and Bristol City in 1909, the FA Cup finals had been a near Northern and Midland monopoly since Blackburn Olympic had dispatched the Old Etonians in 1883.

The Birmingham postcard publisher, **Scott Russell & Company,** was not slow to realise the potential of souvenirs for these events. The 'Scott Series' included nationwide scenic views, humorous and heraldic cards but not surprisingly local interest featured in large measure. A pair of cards of the local teams, Small Heath (495) and Aston Villa (484), were issued for the 1905 season. Both cards are in a matching 'triangular' pose, with the goalkeeper forming the apex and three rows of full-backs, half-backs and forwards. When Villa reached the FA Cup final that year, Scott Russell re-issued the Aston Villa card, still carrying the same serial number, but overprinted, 'Winners of English Cup'. Their opponents in the final, Newcastle United (505), also feature on a 'Scott Series' card but in a less adventurous design. Further cards were printed after the match including: 'Hampton, who scored the two goals against Newcastle in the final at The Crystal Palace, April 1905' (566), and 'Some Aston Birds, who meant to see the match, The English Cup Final, Crystal Palace, 15 April 1905' (569). The latter, showing a few stray Villa fans stumbling towards the stadium. The following year's final, between Newcastle (957) and Everton (960) also attracted the interest of Scott Russell, who produced a pair of souvenirs, with the team groups above a panoramic vignette of the Crystal Palace arena. More prosaically, the publisher's card number 916B, immortalises the good men of Chesterfield Town, in a real-photographic postcard of the 1905-6 team. What must have been one of the last football cards designed by Scott Russell, was of the 1908 Wolverhampton Wanderers English Cup team, with the players grouped together under the cry, 'Play Up Wolves!' However, the following year, Scott Russell found his own reason to cry, as this 'flamboyant character' was declared bankrupt.

Departing the West Midlands for Lancashire, we encounter the most frequently credited photographer's name on football team postcards during the period 1900 to 1914. Not to be confused with Scott Russell, **R. Scott & Company, Manchester** were photographers and printers. This company were producing small booklets of team groups by 1900, and picture postcards three or four years later. All their cards are half-tone printed issues of rugby league and soccer teams. The postcards are not numbered, and no series titles are printed on the cards, although groupings can be identified by examining the printing styles on the obverse and reverse. The seasons are not usually given, although players' names enable the dates to be pin-pointed with fair accuracy. The cards have little aesthetic appeal, being for the most part simply based on team photographs, although one series attempts a design, insetting players' portraits in circular and oval cartouches. A pair of cards was issued for the 1909

FA Cup final, 'Manchester United (Cup Team)' and 'Bristol City (Cup Team)'. The English, Welsh and Scottish international teams for 1911, are embellished with the rose, leek and thistle respectively. Although most of the teams are from the North and Midlands; Newcastle United, Derby County, West Bromwich Albion, Oldham Athletic, Bradford City, Sheffield Wednesday, Blackburn Rovers, Preston North End, Huddersfield Town, Manchester United *inter alia*; Chelsea, Woolwich Arsenal, Southampton and New Brompton have also been noted. For those eschewing the professional game, Scott was able to supply the Northern Nomads and the exclusive Corinthians.

Fellow Mancunian publisher **John Heath,** unlike Scott, relied on other photographers to provide the original images for his football postcards. Football continued for a while during the early stages of the First World War and the season 1914-15 was played to a conclusion in both League and FA Cup competitions, although the Amateur FA claimed that none of their affiliates kicked the leather during the hostilities. Heath produced a series of half-tone postcards for this last season of regular competition, including: Everton, who ended the campaign as First Division Champions; Oldham Athletic, who were runners-up, one point behind; and Manchester City, one of five teams two points behind Oldham.

Similar to Heath, was the Leeds publisher, **Joe Booth.** Booth was a publisher using photographic originals from lensmen local to the clubs concerned. FA Cup semi-finals seemed a fair bet to Booth, presumably arguing that at least half of his unsold cards could be used again for the final. In 1910, the semi-final opponents, Everton and Barnsley, were published together; as were the cards from 1913, 'Burnley English Cup Team, 1913' and 'Sunderland English Cup Team, 1913'. Civic togetherness also proved a feature of Booth's thinking, with the Liverpool and Everton teams for 1912-13 and the Bradford City and Bradford P.A. sides of 1913-14, paired. Joe Booth's local team, Leeds City, sit proudly with their manager Herbert Chapman before the outbreak of war. Unlawful payments to players during the war-time competitions led to the extinction of Leeds City and the near banning of Chapman from football.

Not all publishers credited themselves by printing trade names on their products, one example being the source of the series which we illustrate in this book in numbers 17 to 20 inclusive. This sequence of twelve cards is a veritable 'Who's Who' of pre-First World War star players and in addition the four cards we reproduce, there are: Charles Buchan, William Meredith, Robert Crompton, Harry Hampton, John Mordue, Jock Simpson, Bert Freeman and Jessie Pennington.

THE LEGACY OF
THE LOCAL PHOTOGRAPHER AND PUBLISHER

On 8 January 1921, **Brighton and Hove Albion,** of the newly-formed League Division Three, met First Division Oldham Athletic in an FA Cup tie at the Goldstone Ground. It was a happy afternoon for Brighton, progressing smoothly into the next round of the competition by four goals to one. Before the game, the various sections of the crowd were treated to the sight of a familiar character, carrying a camera and a wooden board, approach them. When he reached one side of the ground, he stopped to set up his camera and then placed the board (on which could be discerned the words 'Wiles; 25, Prestonville Rd., Brighton' above and below a large number) by the wooden fence, against which the crowd were now pressing. He then returned to his camera, which he aimed at the throng, released the shutter and repeated the procedure at another part of the ground, shooting a fresh group of victims. The following Wednesday, numerous town-centre shops displayed a selection of postcards of the crowd, on sale for a few (old) pence each. Prominent on each card was the numbered board and a caption, 'Cup Tie. Jan.8.1921. (Result. Albion 4 – Oldham 1)'. If a spectator could identify himself in the sea of faces and felt the likeness was not too unkind, then he might purchase a memento of the game to show to grand-children in his dotage. The photographer, G. A. Wiles, was one of two brothers, each active in Brighton just before and after the First World War, conspiring, along with other shutterbugs, to leave Brighton and Hove Albion one of the most photographed football clubs of the period. Whether or not a detailed photographic record of a football club exists, is dependent on the town having busy and energetic local photographers. Brighton was more than generously endowed in this respect.

A fine sequence of team portraits was produced by Carter Brothers and E. Pannell between 1908 and 1913. These real photographic cards were produced each season and give full details of the players' names, so providing a complete pictorial record of the teams for these years. Another local photographer, Foster, was also capturing early Brighton team groups, although his postcards have not the same sharpness, nor do they carry detailed information. Foster's cards slightly predate those of Carter/Pannell, being issued around 1905. Before the First World War, Tom Wiles was producing crowd photographs, a practice that we have seen, was to be continued in the 1920s by his brother. Photographs of match incidents also featured in Tom Wiles' repertoire, typical being, 'Brighton and Hove Albion v Watford. Jan.29.1910. Albion's First Goal'.

Special events brought out a little extra in the postcard publishers. In 1910, when Brighton were the Southern League Champions and winners of the Southern Charity Cup, Carter and Pannell designed a commemorative vertical card in which the players, in oval insets, are clustered around the two trophies, with boxes giving details of goal-scorers and the club's playing record for the

44

LOCAL PHOTOGRAPHERS & PUBLISHERS

45

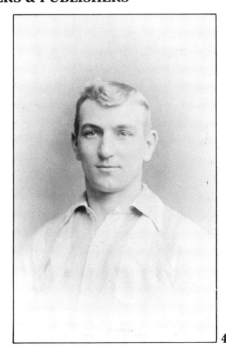

46

DERBY COUNTY FOOTBALL TEAM 1905-6

47

48

NORWICH CITY, 1911-12.

COMER, STRINGFELLOW, WOLSTENHOLME, HAMPSON, BEALE, MELLOR, HARTLEY, W.S.ALDEN, POTTS, PEARSON.
FELL, TAYLOR, CURTIN, BIBBY, WILKINSON, MACKENZIE, KIRKMAN.
J.B.STANSFIELD, JOPLING, INGHAM, POTTER, WOODS, BIRCHALL, C.MILES.(TRAINER)
(MANAGER)

49

WATFORD FOOTBALL CLUB, 1905-6.   [COLE, Photo, Watford.

50

42

51

43

The First CHELSEA Team To Beat ASTON VILLA, Oct 25th 1913.

Tottenham Hotspur FC
1905-6

Souvenir of . .
Benefit Match

GIVEN BY THE DIRECTORS OF THE

BIRMINGHAM FOOTBALL CLUB

❄   ❄

TO

AMBROSE HARTWELL.

FOR MORE THAN FIVE YEARS' LOYAL SERVICE.

April 7th, 1906

54

Swindon's Pride.

55

NORTHAMPTON TOWN FOOTBALL CLUB. SEASON 1907 = 1908.

T. Drennan.   G. Cooch.   Hy. Benson.
Mr. H. Foyle. (Hon. Financial Sec.)   H. Tirrell.   D. McCartney.   F. McDiarmid.   R. C. Brittain.   R. Murrell. (Trainer)
Mr. H. Chapman. (Manager) G. Badenoch. E. Didymus. J. Platt. G. F. Lessons. Mr. H. Springthorpe. E. Freeman. Mr. A. Jones. (General Sec.)
Copyright.   GREENWAY. Northampton.

56

45

57

58

59

GAINSBOROUGH TRINITY, 1904-5.

Caldicott, Whittlam, trainer, W. Eyre, director, Thompson, Bagshaw, Hempsall, T. H. Prescott, C. Gilbert, director, T. Lobley, director, F. M. Walker, Hall, Jenkinson, Turner, Langham, Milson, Dixon, F. Foxall, Foxall.

60

BROMLEY F.C. 1910-11. WINNERS OF THE F.A. AMATEUR CUP.

61

VIVIAN J. WOODWARD.
Tottenham Hotspur F.C. and England's Centre Forward, 1903-4.
Published by Walter Henry, 11, Prince's Street, Westminster, S.W.   Copyright.

62

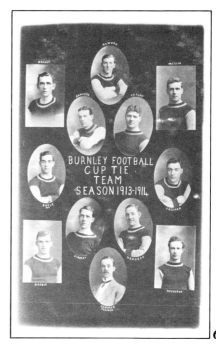

BURNLEY FOOTBALL
CUP TIE
TEAM
SEASON 1913-1914

63

47

SOUTHAMPTON FOOTBALL TEAM, 1905-6.

64

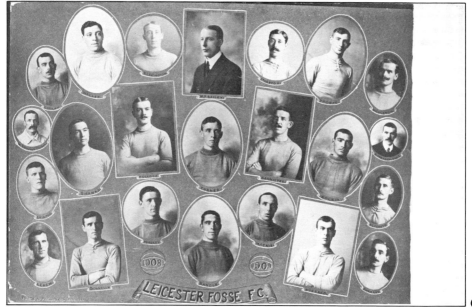

LEICESTER FOSSE F.C.

65

48

44 Furniss Photo, Sheffield – '"Wednesday" 1905-6'.

45 Furniss Photo, Sheffield – 'The English Football Association Cup'. Proudly draped in Wednesday's colours following their 1907 defeat of Everton. This trophy was replaced in 1911, by the present pot, being presented to the old hacker, Lord Kinnaird.

46 Furniss Photo, Sheffield – 'H. Chapman'. Harry was the younger brother of Herbert, and a rather more gifted player. He died in 1916 aged 36, shortly after his wife, leaving their children orphans. This card was issued in 1907 as part of a set to commemorate the club's FA Cup success. These three cards are typical of the local photographer's work. Issued in small quantities for parochial consumption, they are becoming increasingly difficult to find, and provide a unique pictorial record.

47 Derwent series, J. Harwood, Derby – 'Derby County Football Team 1905-6'. 'Dear Mr H. This is our football team. We see some ripping matches, that is when we can get off. Bloomer is the 2nd from the left of the PC. He is a champion you ought to see him. C.'

48 W. Avenell & Co, Brighton – 'Brighton & Hove Albion Football Club 1904-5'.

49 Hayward Kidd, Photo, Norwich – 'Norwich City 1911-12'.

50 Coles Photo, Watford – 'Watford Football Club 1905-6'.

51 Irving Photo, Barnsley – 'The Yorkshire Rose. English Cup Final, April 23rd 1910'. Barnsley's FA Cup final appearances in 1910 and 1912 produced some of the most inspired football postcards of the Golden Age. Alas, in 1910 the Yorkshire Rose wilted in the replayed game at Everton, where Newcastle's fine pre-First World War side recorded their only FA Cup success in five attempts.

52 'The First Chelsea Team to Beat Aston Villa, Oct 25th 1913'. Publisher uncredited. A two-faced compliment following their victory by 2-1.

53 Jones Bros, Postcard Publishers, Tottenham – 'Tottenham Hotspur FC 1905-6'.

54 Birmingham Football Club – 'Souvenir of Benefit Match to Ambrose Hartwell, April 7th 1906'.

55 Protheroe & Simons, Photo, Swindon – 'Swindon Town FC's "Championship" Team 1910-11'. The Southern League Shield was one of football's major prizes before 1920, and the Town were indeed 'Swindon's Pride'.

56 Greenway, Northampton – 'Northampton Town Football Club. Season 1907-1908'. The omnipresent Herbert Chapman and his Northampton side, with whom he would soon enjoy his first managerial success, winning the Southern League the following season.

57 Wakefield Photo, Brentford – 'Brentford 1904-5'.

58 Bradford Park Avenue (RIP) 1907-8. This season gave the Yorkshiremen an identity crisis, being adopted by the Home Counties. They applied to the Football League, where they failed to secure the votes. Promptly applied to the Southern League, and were admitted. They played one season in the South before finding more natural playmates in the Football League the following year.

59 Fred Shaw, Photo, Rotherham – 'Rotherham County FC'. Midland League Champions third year running in 1913–14.

60 Caleb Smith, Lincoln – 'Gainsborough Trinity 1904–5'. A Football League side before the First World War, non-League since 1912.

61 'Bromley FC, 1910–11'. Uncredited publisher. FA Amateur Cup winners, beating Bishop Auckland 2–1 at Herne Hill.

62 Walter Henry, Westminster – 'Vivian J. Woodward, 1903–4'. An architect by profession, Woodward played as an amateur for Tottenham, Chelsea and England, helping England win the Olympic Games' football competition in 1908 and 1912. Woodward has here found a novel use for the old school tie – anchoring his generous-sized shorts.

63 W. W. Smith, Photo, Burnley – 'Burnley Football Cup Tie Team Season 1913–1914'. Burnley won this valedictory Crystal Palace FA Cup final, scoring the only goal in the game against Liverpool.

64 F. G. O. Stuart – 'Southampton Football Team 1905–6'.

65 Phillips & Co, Leicester – 'Leicester Fosse FC 1908–09'.

1909–10 season. When the club defeated the 1910 Football League Champions, Aston Villa, in the Charity Shield, Pannell issued a similar card showing the team for 1910–11, but this time, with the third trophy added to the other two. After the war, G. A. Wiles produced portrait postcards of individual players. One series, for the 1921–22 season, appears solemn and funereal, with the head-and-shoulder portraits set against sombre black backgrounds. FA Cup ties often inspired something different, usually a vertically designed card, with the Brighton players in circular or oval cartouches, the date of the game, the name of the opposition and a space for the result of the match. After the mid-1920s we notice the cards credited to the Brighton Camera Exchange, a trade name believed to be of G. A. Wiles and two partners, although the basic style of the cards remains the same. During the 1930s, the trade title is printed as Deane, Wiles and Miller, a firm enduring until well after the Second World War.

Any historian of Brighton and Hove Albion has an embarrassing wealth of early photographic material and thanks to the postcard format, much of it has been preserved down the years in family albums and private collections. We might add that Brighton also hosted publishers producing early collotype and gravure postcards of the football team, including W. Avenell & Co, Thos. Donovan & Son and the Mezzotint Co.

One football historian who has availed himself of the postcard heritage of his team, is Grenville Firth in his book *The Reds – A Pictorial History of Barnsley Football Club*. This volume traces the history of **Barnsley FC** from its pre-historic origins in the 1880s through to the 'Match Of The Day' punditry of the 1980s. It was during the postcard's golden era that Barnsley shook the football world. In two seasons out of three, the Colliers from the Football League Second Division, reached the FA Cup final. In 1910 'Battling Barnsley' ran onto the Crystal Palace turf to be greeted by Lord and Lady Gladstone and the magnificent Newcastle United. This first game between the juggernaut and jaguar ended in a draw at one goal each. It was to be the end of that year's glory for Barnsley, who went down in the replay at Everton by two goals to nil.

The postcard publishers of Barnsley may not have produced the quantities of their Brighton counterparts, but for creative ingenuity they were unsurpassed. Grenville Firth reproduces six cards starring Amos, the lugubrious Barnsley mascot, whose lucky spell saw the team to the 1910 replay, before the Newcastle Magpie finally broke it. The photographer, W. Randall of Peel Street, has Amos and his ever-present donkey standing inside the old FA Cup with 'FINAL 1901–10' on the trophy and in unadulterated Tykese, 'We'em still in it. I tow'd tha' soa!' Irving of Barnsley published another sequence of cards featuring the oft-beleaguered Amos, in the 'English Cup Series'. One card shows Amos fleeing from an umbrella-wielding Mrs Everton, having stolen her toffee. He is carrying a bag of 'Semi-final honours', and defiantly yelling, 'Ah've said all t'way through Ah should gooa to t'Palace'. Another publisher, Fletcher, saw the progress to the 1910 FA Cup final as a series of fights to the death, with a line of graves for the defeated. Headstones carry epitaphs to the deceased, Everton being freshly interred in the semi-final. An empty grave awaits Newcastle in the final, but alas the gravedigger had dug his own plot!

Not all the cards from Barnsley were quite so morbid or manic, Irving for instance producing a quietly composed study for the Newcastle final, of players' portraits encircling the Yorkshire Rose. The same publisher also issued a card for an earlier round, captioned 'Yorkshire's Hope', the design, similar to the other but minus the bloom. Strangely, when Barnsley reached the final again, in 1912, this time actually taking the trophy back to Oakwell after beating West Bromwich Albion in yet another replay, the creative energy of the postcard publishers seemed to have dissipated. There was none of the vitality of two years earlier, although Randall did conjure up an interesting design using the coal metaphor. The card is headed, 'Bright Nuts From Barnsley's Hard Seam', and portrays the players as fuel in a blazing fireplace, adding, 'Guaranteed to give you a hot time, and to last well'. Certainly, they proved too hot for West Brom.

On Barnsley's doorstep, lies the steel centre of **Sheffield** which enjoyed its most successful footballing period during the first seven years of the century. United lost the replayed FA Cup final to Tottenham in 1901 but returned the following year to beat another Southern League club, Southampton, in the final. Their neighbours, Wednesday, imposed their authority on the League Championship by winning the competition in 1903 and 1904. In 1907, Wednesday won the FA Cup, defeating the current holders, Everton, in the final. The 'court' photographer to Sheffield Wednesday was Furniss, aptly named in the city of steel and his studio was in Langsett Road, Sheffield. Photographic postcards were produced from 1905–6, if not earlier, with the 1907 team group posed alongside the FA Cup and the card captioned 'Cup Winners 1907'. A set of individual photographic head-and-shoulder portraits were issued, possibly in connection with the 1907 FA Cup success and the trophy itself was photographed with a caption reminding purchasers that it was eleven years since Wednesday had last won the famed pot. Several later team postcards of the club were sold before the Great War and after the war Furniss took photographs of United as well. As was the case with many of these local photographers, Furniss' work formed the basis for postcards, often collotype or half-tone, published by other firms.

Before leaving Yorkshire we mention the **Bradford** postcard publisher, Walter Scott. This West Riding firm is not strictly a local publisher, producing for example, a large series of scenic views of localities the length and breadth of the country, their output extending over many years. Football is not one of their more noticeable specialisms although Bradford City's FA Cup glory in 1911 did not go unrecognised. A tinted half-tone card was produced with the caption, 'Bradford City AFC. Winners of the English Cup, Season 1910–11', and copyright noted as 'Walter Scott, Church Bank, Bradford'. Other designs include a photographic montage, with the players around the brand new trophy and an uninspired photographic team postcard for the season 1910–11. If the 1930s belonged to Arsenal and the 1920s to Huddersfield, then the Edwardian age was unquestionably the era of **Newcastle United**. League Champions in 1905, 1907 and 1909, they reached the FA Cup final on five occasions in the seven years 1905 to 1911. Amazingly, this near effortless success in reaching the FA Cup final, was converted into only one victory when, as we noted earlier, they overcame Barnsley after a replay. One theory is that their delicate and intricate close-passing game was just unsuited to the lush turf at the Crystal Palace, where a more direct approach would perhaps have paid off. They were without doubt though, one of the greatest teams in the game's history. Their sides were mainly a brew of Scottish and English talent, with the tartan influence of Aitken, Howie, Lawrence, Low, McColl, McWilliam, Orr and Templeton, blending with the English craft of Carr, Gosnell, Rutherford, Shepherd, Stewart and Veitch. The Irish full-back, McCracken, was acquired from Distillery in 1905, to complete the alcoholic metaphor.

The publisher, Gladstone Adams of Whitley Bay, was producing postcards of Newcastle United before the First World War and still prospering after the Second. One particularly attractive series, features players of the 1911–12 season, with individual portraits in oval frames, below which stand two magpies, cigarettes hanging from their beaks and together, holding a riband on which the player's name appears. Several team line-ups from before the Great War are credited to Adams, as is a later series of portraits of some early 1950s Newcastle players. Another local photographer associated with early century postcards of Newcastle United is J. Taylor of Carrick Street, Newcastle. One series of black and white oval portraits reproduces facsimile signatures in the bottom right-hand corner and includes the players: Higgins, Howie, Lawrence, McWilliam, Shepherd and Veitch. Taylor was on hand to photograph incidents during the 1908 FA Cup semi-final at Anfield, when the Magpies scored six goals against Fulham. He subsequently published a series of photographic postcards to celebrate this slaughter. The company of Ruddock Ltd, from Newcastle-on-Tyne, produced a generous selection of postcards, ranging over several subject areas and intended for wide distribution but their series of local interest cards qualifies them for inclusion in this chapter. Typical is a head-and-shoulders card of the Scottish international wing-half Andrew Aitken.

Another fine Newcastle half-back was Aitken's Scottish international colleague, Peter McWilliam. During the 1912–13 season, McWilliam donned his managerial hat with **Tottenham Hotspur**. Spurs were one of the giants of the South before the Great War, winning the FA Cup from the Southern League in 1901 and gaining promotion to Division One in their first Football League season, 1908–9. They played in the First Division up to the outbreak of war, when they ended the 1914–15 season bottom of their Division. Peter McWilliam saw Spurs to promotion again on the resumption in 1919–20 and the following year, he proudly watched Arthur Grimsdell receive the FA Cup from King George V.

53

The Spurs of those pre-First World War years were depicted on real photographic postcards published by 'Jones. Bros. Tottenham', sometimes credited as, 'F. W. Jones, Postcard Publisher'. Team groups on sepia cards exist from c1904 to 1913-14, as do a series of full-length players' photographs, including Vivian Woodward for the season 1906-7 and Fanny Walden, who arrived in 1913. The Jones cards are also found of players and teams during the 1920s.

Before the First World War, locally published postcards appear to be mostly credited to 'F. W. Jones' or 'Jones Bros.' but during the 1920s, team groups are also found, inscribed, 'Official Photo, Crawford, Edmonton'. Crawford cards of individual players' portraits were produced, starting from the 1919-20 season and club line-ups were also issued for several years from 1919 onwards. Players appearing in the Crawford series include: Bliss, Seed, Whitton, Walden, Walters, Skinner, Jaques, Sage, Jennings, Findlay and Hargreaves.

The South London photographers, J. Russell & Sons of **Crystal Palace**, published several postcards of that club during the Edwardian years, including a team group of 1905-6, the season that the present club was founded by a number of workers from the Crystal Palace itself. Russell also produced a card of the following year's team, which gained admission to the Southern League, where it stayed until becoming founder-members of the newly created Division Three (South) in 1920, winning that League in its inaugural season. One particularly interesting design used by Russell for individual players' portraits at this time, was of a large football 'framing' head-and-shoulder studies. A typical card having the caption, 'Woodger, Crystal Palace Football Team'. Woodger, later moved to Lancashire, where he won an England cap in 1911, whilst with Oldham Athletic. Another Palace player featuring in a different series of cards by this publisher was the goalkeeper, Hewitson. Like Woodger, he joined Oldham and played in that club's first Football League game in 1907 and the following season he also played in Tottenham's League baptism. This latter series was issued c1906, perhaps commemorating their elevation to Southern League status, at a time when that combination included powerful teams. Twelve cards were issued, depicting their first team players.

The West London photographer, Wakefield, is well-known to collectors of topographical views of that area. His premises were at one time in **Brentford**, and later he moved to the Mall, Ealing. Several team groups of Brentford FC were issued from c1904, usually in half-tone printing rather than glossy photographs. Wakefield's novel approach to identifying players in a group line-up, was to overprint their names on the individual player's shirt, rather than list all the names together at the bottom of the card. Brentford, like Crystal Palace, were original members of the Third Division in 1920 and played in that Division in 1924-25 when Wakefield produced a set of glossy sepia photographic postcards of at least seventeen players, each card naming the player and giving his position. It was not a happy season for the Bees, finishing the year just four points above the bottom club, Merthyr Tydfil.

The Shakespeare Press were printers with premises in Hinkley Street, **Birmingham**. Their output of football postcards was not overwhelming but an acceptable, if uninspired, set of West Midlands cards was issued in 1912 of the teams: West Bromwich Albion, Aston Villa, Birmingham and Wolverhampton Wanderers. This publisher is also noted as having published a souvenir of Sunderland's 1913 FA Cup final team. Rather more inspired, were a set of cards offered *c*1905 by the 'Birmingham Novelty Co (Art Publishers)' in their 'Football Celebrities' series. The series consists of coloured head-and-shoulder portraits of several Birmingham area players, including from Aston Villa: Spencer, George, Wilkes, Bache and Leake. From West Bromwich, where Wilkes kept his photographic studio, are Hadley, Randle and Dorsett. Small Heath were the poor relations of the Second City, living constantly in the shadow of their neighbours at Villa Park. Their representatives in the series include: Green and Stokes. We discussed another Birmingham publisher, Scott Russell, in the last chapter.

By its nature, the subject matter of this chapter could be extended to embrace every town and city that boasts a leading football club. Space naturally limits discussion to a selected few. The examples chosen, have been of photographers and publishers, at least some of whose cards, present-day collectors have a realistic chance of finding. Most of the cards produced by local people have tended to remain in the areas concerned, although naturally, others have been posted far and wide, since that was, and is, the chief rôle of a postcard. Local collectors, then, have a far better chance than the general collector, of finding these strictly parochial and civic depictions. A greater possibility exists of locating F. G. O. Stuart cards of **Southampton FC**, or Stephen Cribb cards of **Portsmouth**, on the South Coast, than in the East Midlands, where Caleb Smith was publishing early team squads of **Lincoln** and **Gainsborough Trinity**.

The importance of the local photographer is without question. His work not only gave him pictorial images to sell under his own imprint, but often provided the bases of postcards sold by the giants such as Raphael Tuck and Valentine. To those interested in the history of Association Football, the lack of early pictorial records of some clubs, makes one thankful for the photographic overkill inflicted on others. Guilty of such overkill, as well as those discussed already, we might also accuse W. E. Turton of **Huddersfield**, capturing the Town players before the Great War and Herbert Chapman's wizards of the 1920s. There was W. H. Duncan of **Hull**, providing a detailed record of Hull City teams before and after 1914 and W. Whiffen of Poplar, shooting the **Millwall** Lions of the Twenties. In recent years, local history and topographical postcards have proved themselves among the most avidly sought by British collectors. Regional postcard collectors clubs have sprouted up all over the country and many study groups have set themselves the task of compiling detailed listings of the cards issued by local publishers. It is only as the fruits of this research become available that we will know the full debt of gratitude that social historians owe to these early cameramen and printers.

A THROW IN.

66

A SOUND DEFENCE.

67

A SPILL.

68

A NEAT PASS.

69

70

WELL CLEARED.

GOAL.

71

ALEX. SMITH, Rangers.
is an Ayrshire lad, who gained his experience with Darvel. He has got five caps against England, and is an outside left with fine speed, good temper, and never been known to funk under any circumstances. He was born in 1874.

72

"KENTISH INDEPENDENT" FOOTBALL CARTOON.

BURY
WOOLWICH ARSENAL
JANUARY 20th, 1902.
Result: Arsenal 2, Bury 1

Alas, poor "Bury" I knew him well,
The poor chap 'ad to chuck it,
He tried to put me down, but lo,
'Twas he who kicked the bucket.

73

74

ASTON VILLA FOOTBALL GROUND.

75

76

MANCHESTER CITY.

yours to hand

77

Football Celebrities.
A. RANDLE
(West Bromwich Albion)

78

STOKE.

79

FOOTBALL GROUND, LEYTON

80

BLACKBURN ROVERS FOOTBALL TEAM 1904—1905.

81

82

CHAMPIONS OF THE SOUTHERN LEAGUE 1910-11.

ENGLISH CUP HOLDERS. 1910-11.

PLAY UP CITY.!

N.C.F.C.

83

Everton

GOODISON PARK GROUND LIVERPOOL

84

FAMOUS FOOTBALL TEAMS

NOTTS

COUNTY

85

Outside Newcastle United Football Ground after the Match.

86

59

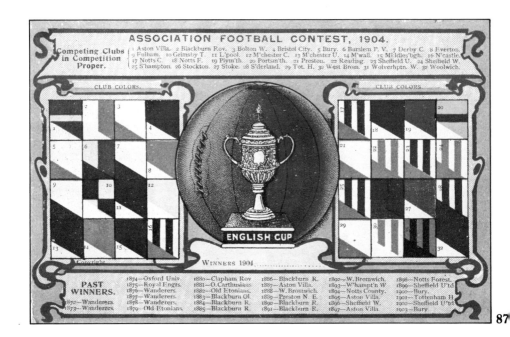

WOLVERHAMPTON WANDERERS

MORRIS · SCOTT · TAYLOR · GALLEY · CULLIS · GARDINER · McINTOSH · WESTCOTT · DORSETT · BURTON · MAGUIRE

The English Cup Team, 1939

90

91

92

93

94

95

96

97

98

Fondest Birthday Wishes

May you have a glorious day,
Pleasures more than words can say,
And may your future prove to be
Happier than ever, Dear, for thee.

99

FOOTBALL.
Talk not of war's alarms;
Football hath greater charms;
Better than feats of arms,
Are feats of feet.
Let them pour grim be mute
Cavalry those who shout
Goals with roaring boot,
Heroes complete.

100

101

102

103

104

105

106

10

108

66 Misch & Co's 'Football Teams', series No. 4130 (29476) – 'A Throw In'.

67 Misch & Co's 'Football Teams', series No. 4130 (29477) – 'A Sound Defence'.

68 Misch & Co's 'Football Teams', series No. 4130 (29478) – 'A Spill'.

69 Misch & Co's 'Football Teams', series No. 4130 (29479) – 'A Neat Pass'.

70 Misch & Co's 'Football Teams', series No. 4130 (29480) – 'Well Cleared'.

71 Misch & Co's 'Football Teams', series No. 4130 (29481) – 'Goal'. A set of six chromolithographic studies from the artist Fred S. Howard. The players' stances are wooden, and the atmosphere, Corinthian.

72 W. Collins, Sons & Co Ltd – 'Herriot' series – 'Alex Smith, Rangers'.

73 Molyneux, Woolwich 'Molyneux' series, No. 23 – '"Kentish Independent" Football Cartoon. Bury v Woolwich Arsenal'. From a set of 30 cards celebrating the Gunners' first season in Division One, 1904–5.

74 T. & G. Mackenzie, Athletic Outfitters, Edinburgh – 'Bobby Walker'. The oft-capped Edwardian Scottish international.

75 W. H. Whittingham, B'ham – 'Aston Villa Football Ground'. Card posted September 1904.

76 J. Sharples, Marple, 'Roman' series – 'Imperial Hotel, Headquarters, Manchester United FC'.

77 'Manchester City'. 'Write-away' series of club colours. Publisher uncredited. Artist, 'FR'.

78 Birmingham Novelty Art Co, Art Publishers, 'Football' series – 'Football celebrities. A. Randle (West Bromwich Albion)'.

79 B. B. (Birn Bros) series, No. G.11 – 'Stoke'. The series also includes Bristol City, Notts County and Preston North End.

80 Hubbard & Son, Leyton – 'Football Ground, Leyton'.

81 J. Neville, Blackburn – 'Blackburn Rovers Football Team 1904–1905'.

82 'W. J. Oakley (Corinthians) "Dribbling"' – Publisher uncredited. Early chromographed card c1898–1900, blemished by heavy postmark.

83 Hayward T. Kidd's series – 'Play up City!' Norwich City's two goals for 1910–11 – Southern League and English Cup – eyed by optimistic canary.

84 Dainty series – 'Everton'. Postally used April 1905.

85 The Wrench series, No. 10714 – 'Famous Football Teams. Notts County'. Posted January 1905.

86 R. Gibson – 'Outside Newcastle United Football Ground After the Match'. c1910.

87 N. & C., London – 'English Cup. Association Football Contest, 1904'.

88 HJS Copyright. A. W. C., London, No. 1000 – 'The Fight for the Championship! Who will lift it? 1904–5'. Answers presumably on a postcard. The current champs, Sheff. Wed., perched loftily on a huge football.

89 Geo E. Lee, Wolverhampton, the 'Wulfruna' series – Wolverhampton Wanderers.

The English Cup Team, 1939' Identical design to a card issued for the Wolves' 1908 FA Cup final.

90 British Art Co, Britart series 129 – 'Our Definite Goal'. To war and propaganda.

91 'Herzlichen Ostergrüss!' – Teutonic bunnies.

92 Muscular Christian moralising verse *c*1903. Uncredited publisher.

93 B.B. (Birn Bros) series No. E41 – 'A Run by the Forwards'. One of six action and incident cards from leading venues.

94 'An Exciting Moment'. Uncredited publisher.

95 C. W. Faulkner & Co, series 327B – 'Association Football: "Goal!"'. Chromographed card *c*1905 after G. D. Rowlandson.

96 Philco Pub Co, series 2176A – 'A Shot at Goal'.

97 Aldine series 228 – uncaptioned soccerette.

98 Misch & Co's, 'The Footballers' series, No. 445 (29517) – 'On the Ball'. From a set of six similar studies. Postally used 1911.

99 'Fondest Birthday Wishes'. uncredited publisher *c*1925.

100 Valentine's series – 'More moralising stanzas'. Posted March 1906.

101 Wildt & Kray, series 596 – 'Foul'. *c*1905 after Reg Carter. From a series of several soccer studies by this artist.

102 Raphael Tuck & Sons' 'Oilette' Football Incidents, series 1746 – 'Charged Through'. Perhaps an erstwhile Nat Lofthouse! Tuck also published this set in monochrome.

103 Langsdorff & Co, No. 690 – 'The Captain'. After Kinsella. This rosy-cheeked hacker was also calamity-prone in cricket and cycling, his 'sister' starring in the tennis rôle.

104 'España 82'. From a set of attractive souvenirs of the multi-million peseta finals.

105 'Alitalia Challenge Cup'. Anglo-Italian inter-league semi-professional tournament.

106 Fisa, publishers – 'Liverpool the Team for All Seasons'.

107 Coffer, publishers – 'Emlyn Hughes. Liverpool FC and England'. *c*1970.

108 Coffer, publishers – 'Manchester City FC'. *c*1970.

THE ART OF FOOTBALL
VICTORIAN PAINTERS AND EDWARDIAN POSTCARDS

Living in the last quarter of the twentieth century, we are prisoners of a technology that saturates us in graphic imagery. From early in the morning to late in the evening, pictorial images constantly assault our senses. We take for granted the cathode-ray tube, offering instantaneous glimpses of events far and wide; of Papal visits, royal tours, floods and wars, music and sport. It is impossible to pick up a magazine or newspaper without finding the photographic or artistic illustration. The visual image, either still or moving, is a major ingredient of our environment. It is perhaps difficult for us to imagine a time when things were not so, although it is only since the 1950s that television has become the powerful force that it is. We have become so conditioned to the beaming of pictures from the other side of the world, and indeed from other worlds, that the impact of a simple photograph or drawing on an Edwardian or Victorian forefather would be hard for us to understand. His world was far more a world of words, either spoken or written. A small line drawing or painting was an enrichment to his experience, in a way that it would not be to ours.

With the introduction of the larger standard-sized pictorial postcards after 1899, the ordinary person, who did not normally have access to paintings and pictures, found a new cheap source of graphic art and he acquired these 'masterpieces in miniature' with relish. In previous chapters we have already seen how the postcard publishers used the photographic plate and negative as a basis for producing cards of scenes and celebrities. The postcard artist, with trained eye, skilled brush, and often fevered imagination, was the other inspiration.

The popular notion of postcard art is of beleaguered husbands, pneumatic wives and suggestive captions. Certainly the saucy seaside card exists in abundance, but there is rather more to it than that. One guess is that as many as 20,000 artists designed for postcards, although this statistic includes many continental artists, unknown outside the most specialist of circles. The 'Art Nouveau' movement at the turn of the century produced some of the most exquisitely crafted art to appear on pictorial postcards, although the British artist generally offered a more prosaic depiction. The comic postcard is not, despite its reputation, totally without subtlety and in the next chapter we will discuss how this typically British art-form took a sideways glance at football. Here we take a more head-on look at football postcard art.

Association football can be strictly dated from October 1863, when the FA held its inaugural meeting. The founding fathers had played football at the Public Schools, where each establishment claimed its own set of rules, determined in part by the facilities available for athletic sports. The open spaces at Rugby, for example, permitted an open, running game, whereas at Charterhouse, the close confines of the cloisters necessitated a more restrictive, dribbling contest. It was to overcome these differences in rules of play and agree on a common code, that the FA was founded. Until the early 1880s, the game of Association Football was dominated, on and off the field, by the Public Schools and their alumni. The de-gentrification came with the improvement in play by the working men of the North and Midlands, when, for example, in 1883, the artisan players from Blackburn Olympic, defeated the 'old school tie', personified by the Old Etonians, in that year's FA Cup final. By 1900 the game was the sport of the masses, rather than a recreation simply of the privileged, although the finest amateur players could still find places in the international teams and the Corinthians were more than a match for most of the professional elevens.

Despite the increasing importance of the working-class game, the later Victorian artists, almost without exception, portrayed football in all its Corinthian colours. It was to them gentlemanly, dignified, noble and character-forming; if at times, bracing and vigorous. Most artists represented on 'serious' Edwardian soccer postcards, were Victorian-trained and they inherited, then imparted, this idealistic view of football. Because early photographic emulsions were usually too slow to capture the high-speed action of football incidents, it is not easy to find many photographic studies, as distinct from artistic impressions, of matches before the turn of the century, although the Badminton Library did produce an engraving based on a photograph for its 1887 edition. This incident, often reproduced in football histories, shows the West Bromwich Albion centre-forward, Bayliss, rising to head the ball during the FA Cup final of 1887 and was proudly claimed by Badminton to be the first such illustration. They were no doubt, aware of how unconvincing the artists' drawings of match incidents had been in such up-market weeklies as *The Illustrated London News*, and *The Graphic*, when the quickness of the action had deceived the artists' sense of perspective and posture, just as the earlier horse-racing painters – Stubbs, Herring and Frith – had been tricked into splaying their horses legs to exaggeration.

We have already encountered the publisher, **Raphael Tuck & Sons,** in connection with their series of football players and teams, but this company's range of cards was nothing if not wide and varied. Their most well-known generic title was for cards based on artist-drawn and painted originals, issued under the designation 'Oilette'. The 'Oilette' cards first appeared in 1903, and were produced for many years and in vast quantities, using the work of numerous artists including A. R. Quinton, whose paintings-on-postcards of scenic British views are keenly collected today; Lance Thackeray, whose brush and palette took a more whimsical direction; and **S. T. Dadd.**

Dadd was a minor Victorian painter, whose inclusion in this book is based on a series of football action drawings that Tuck issued, both in Dadd's original monochrome black and white form, and also in an 'Oilette' version, after colouring. Dadd worked from the late 1870s until the early 1890s, and his football drawings are imbued with the typical Victorian characteristics outlined earlier. The monochrome series, 'Football Incidents', has the Tuck number

1203 and consists of six cards, three with the parenthesis 'Association', the other three carrying the epithet 'Rugby'. Two of the six cards are titled 'Oxford v Cambridge', one each for Association and Rugby and it looks as though these university games inspired the other incidents as well. The card captioned 'Charged Through', illustrates a muscular challenge on the goalkeeper, who is clutching the ball and, wearing a suitably pained expression. The third soccer card, 'A Close Shave', shows an attack on goal that, despite their gentlemanly values and principles of fair play, looks suspiciously like a good old plebeian 'offside'. The other Rugby cards are given as, 'A Try', which portrays an unquestioned three points, and 'Nearly In', depicting as fine a flying tackle into touch as one could hope to see. The 'Oilette' series has the Tuck number 1746 and the cards all carry identical captions to the non-coloured series. At this point we might briefly mention the publisher **S. Hildesheimer & Co**, who also issued at least one of these Dadd cards. The card designated 'Oxford v Cambridge (Association)', by Tuck, was published by Hildesheimer, with the same caption, although the other titles await discovery, if indeed they were published at all.

Pictures rely on medium as well as message. There is general agreement among those who have seen and handled postcards from the various periods, that whatever the subject-matter, one of the finest printing techniques for colour reproduction was the early chromolithographic process. It was a lengthy and expensive procedure, but the final product had a richness and warmth that has never been surpassed. The most expert chromolithography was achieved in the German States, and many early cards bear the message, 'Printed in Germany', or 'Chromographed in Saxony'. During the 1890s many Continental cards proclaimed 'Grüss Aus', beside chromographed vignettes of spas, resorts, towns and cities. These early Grüss Aus cards are among the most sought-after 'chromos', but they are not the only ones.

The publisher **Misch & Co** is best remembered today for a long series of early reproductions of famous paintings by many of the Old Masters, issued in conjunction with the German publisher Stengel. Similar colour reproduction was achieved by Misch and Stengel in two series of football studies by the artist **Fred S. Howard**. The poses are wooden, static and totally unconvincing but this notwithstanding, the excellence of the colour printing alone makes these cards worth collecting. Misch cards often carry two serial numbers – a Misch series number, followed by Stengel's own serial number. The 'Football Teams' series has Misch number 4130, with each card given a Stengel number from 29476 to 29481 inclusive. Starting with 'A Throw In' (29476), we score the 'Goal' (29481) via 'A Sound Defence' (29477), 'A Spill' (29478), 'A Neat Pass' (29479) and 'Well Collared' (29480). The other series has an earlier Misch number but later Stengel numbers. 'The Footballers', series number 445, has Stengel numbers 29513 to 29518 inclusive, and consists of six vertical designs of equally lifeless and stiff-limbed athletes but with the same high-quality Stengel printing.

The **Philco Publishing Company** was based in Holborn Place, London and if their colour reproduction did not reach the standard of Stengel and Misch, they were responsible for one of the most charming sets of artist-created football postcards. Their series 2176, is based on six oil paintings by the artist '**J.W.G.**', the cards being individually allotted a different letter of the alphabet, with serial identifications running from 2176A to 2176F. Each card shows a youthful and rosy-cheeked footballer against an idyllic woodland setting. 'Just Signed On' (2176E) has a ready and determined player, one hand in pocket, the other holding a football against his side and set for the fray. The red-shirted goalkeeper in 'A Surprise Shot' (2176C) looks anxious, but well-positioned to deal with the crises. A welcome break at 'Half Time' (2176D) for an exhausted battler, leaning against a stone wall, with natty red cap still not dislodged from his blond curls. Skills from the coaching manual in 'A Run Down The Field' (2176F) and 'Heading The Ball' (2176B), with both the players keeping their eyes fixed firmly on the ball, whilst holding a well-balanced posture. Whether or not a 'Shot At Goal' (2176A) is converted into a score, we are left to ponder.

The full standard-sized cards permitted by the Universal Postal Union, were of dimension 140 mm by 89 mm and we have already noted the increased opportunities for picture postcard design that were enjoyed, following Britain's accepting these larger cards in November 1899. Before this date, cards posted for delivery in Britain were usually of 'court size' dimensions (115 mm by 89 mm), a size accepted by the British postal authorities in 1895. It is very unusual to find pictorial football postcards in anything less than standard size, although football clubs had used earlier, smaller postcards with a printed message, often advising players of selection and travel arrangements. These were, however, just overprinted plain postcards. Football picture postcards do not emerge in any numbers until about 1902, when the first team line-ups and players' portraits appear.

One exception to this is a very fine set of under-sized (ie less than full UPU standard size) cards issued by an uncredited publisher in the late 1890s. One of these cards is shown in this book (see illus No. 82), where we reproduce a chromo-vignette of W. J. Oakley, the Corinthian and England full-back and Oxford Athletics Blue. Fellow Corinthian, Charles Wreford-Brown, the England centre-half of the 1890s, features on a card in which he is seen galloping after the ball, the artist, as in the Philco series, adopting a rural, sylvan background. Further cards in the series, set various other international players, such as Derby's John Goodall, against equally incongruous backdrops. This series can lay claim to be one of, if not the, first football postcard sets issued in Britain, although the high quality chromolithography was a product of the German printers.

We finally mention another excellent chromolithograph, this time from **C. W. Faulkner & Company** in their series 327, with the caption 'Association Football: "Goal!"'. The artist, **G. D. Rowlandson**, creates a successful attack, rounded off by the thunderous drive into the net (see illus No. 95). The companion cards in the series illustrate equally momentous incidents from various other sports.

Association football has a meagre portfolio of paintings, engravings and prints. The artists and engravers commissioned by the *Boy's Own Paper*, *Graphic* and *The Illustrated London News*, offered the late Victorians an unreal and impressionistic glimpse into the game. The Edwardian postcard artists usually provided their public with similar. In the next section we meet some of those heretical painters who viewed the sacred sport with less than untrammelled reverence.

IT'S A FUNNY OLD GAME
SOCCER AND THE COMIC POSTCARD (1900–1914)

The humorous postcard, with its parade of overdeveloped women, cowering husbands, angry policemen and thinly veiled sexual innuendo, is the characteristically British postcard art-form. Before the advent of the continental package-tour, the saucy postcard was a key and integral part of the traditional seaside holiday, alongside the bucket-and-spade, stick of rock, paddling father and formidable landlady. Like most postcards, the comic designs enjoyed a Golden Age after the turn of the century and then degenerated after the First World War, so that George Orwell was moved to write a defence of the artist **Donald McGill**, in the September 1941 edition of *Horizon* magazine. McGill was accused of being vulgar, rather than funny and his hurriedly drawn and gaudily coloured sketches were claimed to be without merit, although Orwell argued that McGill's was an art of the people – a 'folk-art'. McGill was the quintessential British postcard artist and because he was active for so many years – from 1904 until shortly before his death in 1962 – his personal development reflects the changes in comic postcard art in the movement as a whole.

Before the First World War, humorous postcards took a wry look at many facets of life and were not restricted to the earthy and suggestive themes of later years. The designs were not without artistic quality and the printing was of a standard that would bear comparison with the finest cards of any genre. Donald McGill started his postcard drawing in 1904 when he sketched a few amusing studies on the backs of plain cards for a sick nephew. The **Pictorial Postcard Company**, in their 'Empire Series (E.S.)', published a set of six cards of football in 1905. These cards, in the 'E.S. series 135', were in what postcard collectors have come to call 'Write-Away' format. The name derives from a series by **Raphael Tuck**, titled 'Write Away', in which a pictorial vignette appears next to the space for the message, with the first few words of the communication printed on the card, the sender having to complete the rest. Tuck's 'Write Away' series 758, for example, includes the view of a goalkeeper stretching to catch the ball, the opening line of the message printed as 'Just in time'. The McGill series shows soccer and rugby action, each printed line beginning 'Dear' followed by a space for the name of the addressee and the introductions: 'I must apologise'; 'Caught the post'; 'Tried very hard'; 'Hope to get over'; 'Shall I be considered pressing'; 'Quite a mistake on my part'. The various introductions are each amusing word-plays on their accompanying drawings. The following year McGill issued a set of cricket cards through the same publisher. Donald McGill went on to produce nearly 10,000 postcard designs for several different publishers, but there seems to be general agreement that his finest work belongs to the early period.

Tom Browne (often simply signed 'Tom B.') was a contributor to *Punch* magazine and an exhibitor at the Royal Academy. His vividly coloured and

109

110

THE ART OF FOOTBALL

111

112

I hope to see you soon

I was very much worried

A PENALTY !
ONE WAY OF CHEATING
THE GOAL-KEEPER !

115

The Laws of Association Football

" Charging is permiss-
able, but it must
not be violent or
dangerous."

116

Football
on the Brain

117

75

A GOAL KEEPER

I DON'T THINK.

118

A Lucky Save.

11

THE REFEREE
IN THE HANDS OF THE PHILISTINES

120

"HANDS"

1

An Unexpected Attack **122**

After the ball **123**

MAKING UP FOR THE OTHER PLAYERS.

126

FOOTBALL INCIDENTS.
A CLOSE SHAVE (*Association*). *After the black & white drawing, by S. T. DADD.*

127

OXFORD & CAMBRIDGE FOOTBALL

128

FISCAL FOOTBALL

A Good Piece of Head Work.

12

13

109 W. Davidson series No. 25 – 'Prehistoric Football'. After Lawson Wood. Postally used July 1914.

110 Knight Bros Ltd, 'Knight Series', No. 1967 – 'Good Old Soccer'.

111 William Ritchie & Sons Ltd, 'Reliable Series' – 'The Footballer's Crest'. Postally used October 1906.

112 William Collins Sons & Co Ltd, 'Herriot' series – 'Football Phrases Illustrated. A Penalty'.

113 Ernest Nister, series 42 – 'I Hope to see you soon'. An undivided-back 'Write-away'.

114 Aldine series 229 – 'I was very much worried'. After Ralph Rowland. Postally used 1904.

115 Valentine's series – 'A Penalty. One Way of Cheating the Goal-keeper'. Postally used May 1910.

116 Cynicus Publishing Co Ltd – 'The Laws of Association Football'. Wounded football hero created by Cynicus (Martin Anderson) and published by his own company.

117 Cynicus Publishing Co Ltd, No. 11238 – 'Football on the Brain'. A big-headed soccer star published by Cynicus but drawn by another artist. Postally used January 1911.

118 IXL series, Football Studies, series 20,101 – 'A Goal Keeper'. After 'MAC' (Henry Shepheard). Postally used August 1907.

119 Millar & Lang Ltd 'National Series' – 'A Lucky Save'.

120 Millar & Lang Ltd 'National Series', No. 484 – 'The Referee in the Hands of the Philistines'. Postally used March 1908. Millar and Lang produced an immense number of rib-tickling cards and every one, they boasted, printed in Britain.

121 Philco series No. P.S.2588 – 'Hands'. Postally used 1915.

122 Valentine's series – 'An Unexpected Attack'. After Harry Rountree. Postally used April 1906.

123 Davidson Bros, series 2520 – 'After the Ball'. After Tom Browne. Browne issued over 900 cards for Davidson, this musical pun, typical of his wry view of life.

124 Pictorial Postcard Co Ltd, E.S. (Empire Series) No. 3124 – 'Sorry I can't Stop'. After Donald McGill. McGill's was the epitome of British postcard art, not always in the most delicate taste, although this incident appears innocent if somewhat vigorous.

125 Philco series No. 3416A – 'We're Thinking of Dropping this and going in for Limericks'. After Louis Wain. A trio of bruised but smiling footballing felines from the prince of cat-men.

126 Art and Humour Publishing Co Ltd, A & H 'Footer' series No. 769 – 'Making up for the other Players'. After Fred Spurgin. Ungentlemanly conduct?

127 Raphael Tuck & Sons' 'Football Incidents' series 1203 – 'A Close Shave (Association)'. After S. T. Dadd. One of six cards of soccer and rugby published in monochrome (here) and coloured 'Oilette' (see illustration No. 102).

128 S. Hildesheimer & Co Ltd – 'Oxford & Cambridge, Football'. From the same series of drawings by Dadd appearing in the Tuck set. The players, statuesque and noble; the conduct, gentlemanly and Victorian; and the composition, unwitting self-mockery.

129 Raphael Tuck & Sons' 'Fiscal' series, No. 6142 – 'Fiscal Football. A Good Piece of Head Work'. Sport and politics. The football motif taken up by Bradshaw, as Joseph Chamberlain defends his 'goal', by protective trade tariffs against an attack of foreign imports. This card was posted in 1906, the year that Chamberlain was paralysed by a stroke, leaving him an invalid until his death in 1914.

130 Robert Peel Postcard Co, Oxford, Sport series, No. 3 – 'Football'. After 'Nap' c1904.

whimsical studies of the Edwardians at work and play are keenly sought by latter-day postcard collectors and understandably so. He was born in Nottingham in 1870, where he studied art, before moving to London where he co-founded the London Sketch Club. Browne's postcards were issued by several publishers including Tuck, Valentine and Wrench, but his closest association was with the firm of **Davidson Brothers**, who were also linked with other fine comic postcard artists such as John Hassall, Louis Wain and Phil May. It has been speculated that Browne may have had a financial interest in this company, which folded about the time of Browne's death from cancer in 1910. Davidson's sets of cards with numbers 2500 to 2648 were all by Tom Browne and the range took in all aspects of Edwardian life. Domestic situations and sport were particular favourites and so it comes as no surprise to learn that football did not escape his attentions. The envelope to the series No. 2546 declares it to contain 'Six Pictorial Post Cards Designed By Tom Browne, R.I., R.B.A.'. The contents reveal a healthy fun-poking at a game, that has lately been in danger of taking itself rather too seriously. 'A Throw In' shows an angry mob of players and spectators hurling everyone's favourite, the referee, head-first into a nearby pond, whilst 'Head Work' has two combatants both missing the ball, but not each other, in a thunderous crack of heads. 'Fisting Out The Ball' illustrates how the muscular goalkeeper can dispose of both the ball and opposing player at the same time. The Davidson series No. 2633, provides similar fare, with six more hairy incidents. In 'Who'll Volunteer To Get The Ball?' a group of mystified footballers wonder how they are to retrieve the ball, impaled on the horns of a particularly unco-operative and menacing bull. Other Brownesque situations also show what a life-or-death game football actually is.

Probably the most frequently encountered footballer in the postcard dealer's stock is a ginger-haired, red-faced, young smooth-chin wearing a determined expression and red and blue halved shirt. This likeable character was the creation of the Irish artist **Edward ('Pat') Kinsella**. The young sportsman's first appearance was as a cricket star, published by **Langsdorff & Company** in a set of six incidents, later displaying his talents also in cycling, with his 'sister', in yet another series, showing off her tennis skills. The cycling cards are scarce by comparison with the football and cricket, which sold in their hundreds of thousands. Certainly the numbers of surviving cards are consistent with the claim that the cricket sets, sold 250,000 during the first three months. The football sequence (series 690), was equally popular and it is not difficult to make up the set of six by acquiring the individual cards separately.

We have already mentioned the 'Write-Away' style in connection with Donald McGill and Raphael Tuck. The **Aldine** series No. 229, also made use of this device. A set of six cards, each signed by the artist **Ralph Rowland**, and dated 1903, shows several football incidents (usually painful), each accompanied by the opening words of the prospective message. 'It Gives Me Great Pain' is printed by an unfortunate player who has, we are led to believe, received the ball full in the stomach. A generously corpulent goalkeeper, seen flying across the goal, but still failing to stop the shot, is addressing the ball thus, 'I'm Very Sorry I Missed You'. Perhaps most anguished of all is the expression on the face of a red-shirted footballer, pinned to the ground under the weight of a bulky opponent saying 'I Tried Hard To Drop Across You'.

Reginald Carter was an East Anglian artist, whose postcard work started when he was still in his teens, and continued well after the First World War. In 1905, one of the many publishers for whom he worked, **Wildt & Kray**, issued their series 596. The 'star' of the series is a scrawny, under-sized youth, struggling to get the better of a huge football. In 'Goal', the ball carries the luckless footballer into the back of goal, whilst 'The Referee', with whistle in mouth, and 'Billy-Pot' hat on head, signals a score.

No account of comic postcard artists would be complete without at least a passing reference to **Louis Wain**. It was as the creator of hundreds, if not thousands, of animal illustrations, in particular cats in human guise, that he is best remembered. His cats appeared as illustrations in children's books, and then on picture postcards. His was a tragic later life, spending fifteen years in a mental hospital, before his death in 1939. The later drawings grew increasingly manic, although the earlier cat cards have charm and display more restraint. His cats appeared in a whole range of human situations and sports of various kinds featured. Illustration No. 125 in this book shows a feline football card from **Philco**, just one of the many publishers reproducing the work of this gifted but unfortunate artist. The cats have played the match, carry their wounds bravely, but muse (mews?) whether there is a less painful recreation.

Lawson Wood trained at the Slade School of Art and was a friend of Tom Browne. Like Louis Wain, he is well-known today for a series of animal-in-human-situation postcards, although his taste was more simian than feline. During the inter-war years, 'Gran'pop' the chimpanzee involved himself in a variety of incidents, not excluding sport. Another popular series of Wood cards is his 'Prehistoric' sequence. These cards were issued by the publisher Davidson, who as we have seen, also produced many of Tom Browne's drawings. The 'Prehistoric Football' set was published before the First World War, 'A Foul Movement' reminding us that, like their descendants, soccer playing cavemen were not above breaking the rules and each other's heads as well.

Symonds' London Stores, of 128 City Road, were certainly not one of the Golden Age's major publishers, but credit must go to them for an amusing series of postcards carrying cartoons drawn and signed by **R. H. Rahilly,** and dated 1903. In 'Football Expressions. "Claiming a Fowl"', two housewives confront each other, one accusing her foe pointedly with, 'It's my hen', the other, holding the said bird to her side defiantly. Meanwhile, Gussie is a monocled, cigar-smoking, chinless toff, whose thoughts are offered so, 'Oh, no, I nevah play football; I think the costume makes a fellah look so widiculous y'know.'

84

Some artists chose to adopt a nom-de-guerre. **Cynicus** was the Scottish publisher and artist, Martin Anderson. Anderson was one of postcards' more fascinating characters. His drawings were rough, and the satire was biting. He saw himself as 'a reformer, as everybody who pities suffering . . . is a reformer', and some of his fiercest pictorial invective was against hypocrisy. He built himself a castle in the early years of the century, when business was good, and continued to live there after 1916, when his company had failed. He died poor, on his birthday in 1932. His was an original talent and we include two cards in this book from his company. No. 116, 'The Laws of Association Football', was drawn by Anderson and shows a bruised, battered and bandaged footballer. No. 117 is by a different artist, captioned 'Football On The Brain', it portrays a 'big-headed' player and was posted in early 1911.

The **I.X.L.** series included several splendid caricatures by **'Mac'**. The uninitiated are introduced to the arcane mysteries of positional play in the football eleven. 'A Full Back' is, for example, a rear-view of a broad-beamed defender, and 'A Centre Forward' is the man who is hit full in the face with the ball. The other positions receive equally vivid elucidation in this series, which was published some time before 1906.

Valentine & Sons' 'Football' series No. 1 does not credit the artist in a set of studies of the rough-and-tumble of soccer and rugby. 'A Friendly Game, Half Time' treats us to the painful sight of the wounded heroes rubbing ankles, shins, backs and heads in preparation for the resumption of hostilities. 'A Walk Over For The Home Team' shows a fallen player trampled on by the battling factions of both sides. Valentine's 'Souvenir Postcard' trademark appears on the back of another unsigned card posted in 1908, carrying the caption 'Little Binks' First (And Last) Match'. Poor Binks wonders how to dispossess an enormous opponent hurtling down on him at frightening speed. A happier moment in 'Goal !!!' from the same series, where the ecstasy of a score has the players performing jigs and hand-stands. Two Valentine cards signed by the artist **C. K. Cook** in 1903 are respectively titled 'Foul' and 'No Foul'. In the former, the referee, dressed in tartan cap and plus-fours, blows lustily for the infringement, whereas in the latter, the crowd are heartily amused as the poor old referee receives the ball in the stomach, believing himself the victim of an unfair act. More vigorous play in 'What Ho! She Bumps' by the same artist and 'Beg Pardon, Thought You Were The Ball' by **Harry Rountree**, where a myopic footballer kicks his opponent in the seat of the pants, on a card published c1906. 'An Unexpected Attack' by Rountree was also launched by Valentine at the same time.

Valentine's compatriot publisher, **Millar & Lang** of Glasgow, were one of the most prolific producers of postcards during the Edwardian era. All the cards were printed on their own, rather than foreign, presses and so they adopted the title 'National Series' to emphasise this patriotic claim. Their output of comic cards of every theme was enormous and this company has bequeathed the richest source of humorous football postcards. The cards are very seldom signed by the artists, although a young ragamuffin, not dissimilar to Kinsella's urchin, crops up on several cards initialled '**A.A.**'. In 'A Header Into Goal', two such wide-eyed and ragged footballers vie with each other, the one attempting to defend his goal against the other's header. Most of the cards have individual serial numbers, although the same number can occur on different designs, with variations in printing on the backs of the cards. Number 484 for example, shows 'A Hard Worker' forcing his way through a fragile defence, whilst the same number is printed on 'Goal!!!', in which a barn-storming forward crashes his way through a lightweight goalkeeper and equally brittle goalpost. The former card has brown printing on the back, whilst the latter has green. An early unnumbered 'National Series' card depicts a weary player taking a tot of liquid sustenance at 'Half Time', this undivided-back card being posted late in 1903. Advice to potential brides in 'Don't Marry A Footballer', where the unfortunate wife is toe-poked out of bed, with the sleeping, dreaming spouse yelling 'Goal!' Most of this firm's cards were issued singly rather than in sets, although series 2118 has been noted, including 'Brains Versus Beef', with a large-headed footballer pitting his intelligence against the bulk of the brawny goalkeeper, in a contest of mind and matter. Other cards in the set take up a similar theme in 'The Charge Of The Heavy Brigade', and 'It's Weight That Tells', where girth and not guile is clearly the key to success. There is no space here to list all the known cards by this publisher, but despite the large numbers produced, neither artistic skill nor printing quality has been sacrificed and all the cards are colourful and collectable.

Glasgow was and still is, the home of **William Collins, Sons & Company**, who we discussed earlier, in connection with a set of artist's impressions of leading international players. Their output of humorous cards was not nearly so prodigious as their fellow citizens, Millar & Lang, but the 'Herriot Series' (No. 235), 'Football Phrases Illustrated', is worthy of mention. 'A Smart Pass' shows an unshaven pickpocket removing a silk handkerchief from the frockcoat of an unsuspecting gent, whilst 'passing' an already purloined watch to a waiting accomplice. 'A Throw In' should appeal to animal lovers everywhere. A black cat has been attached to a heavy brick and hurled without mercy into the river, by a gloating catophobe. In 'Left Wing', a hungry diner is expectantly carving that portion of a roast-turkey. Similar visual puns are inflicted on 'A Centre Forward', 'A Corner' and 'A Penalty'.

The list of publishers inviting us to smile at soccer is long and it is not possible to describe in detail all their cards in a short chapter. A few cards not included here, appear in the illustrations. Many more await discovery, when perhaps a comprehensive listing can one day be attempted.

FOOTBALL FOR THE MASSES

Association Football at the turn of the century, was not only played at the highest professional level before great multitudes, but the existence of large numbers of pictorial postcards of the Edwardian 'coarse footballer', also testifies to the game's growing appeal as a popular participation sport. Exact statistics are difficult to obtain, but estimates suggest that during the early years of the century, approximately half a million enthusiastic amateur players turned out each week of the season to do battle in fields and parks all over the country. This, at a time when the FA was also claiming about 5,000 registered professional and part-time professional players. Certainly the numbers of surviving postcards bear out these figures, with dozens, if not hundreds, of cards of 'everyman' for each one of a Bloomer or Meredith. Unfortunately, many of these family album cards carry neither captions nor other means of identification, but if the date and affiliation can be determined, they become fascinating items of local history.

Cards of Edwardian school teams are frequently encountered, which is no great surprise, considering the key role of athletic sports and Swedish drill in the curriculum of the elementary schools, introduced via Forster's pioneering Education Act of 1870. During the final twenty years of the last century, school football associations were established in several urban centres, including: South London (1885), Manchester (1890) and Leeds (1896). In 1904 a national governing body was formed, with the founding of the English Schools Football Association.

Religious organisations have a well documented link with football. The Victorian 'Muscular Christians' carried soccer to the industrial centres of Britain, involving themselves with the births of several leading clubs, including Aston Villa, Barnsley, and Everton. Postcards such as 'Garratt Lane Mission Football Club. Winners of Wandsworth Auxiliary League, 1908-9', are typical of those inspired by God's goalpost.

Like the Church, the Army has a long involvement with football. The Royal Engineers of Chatham were losing finalists in the first ever FA Cup final, played in 1872 on the Surrey County cricket ground at the Oval, and an Army Cup was first competed for in 1888-9. During the last decade of the century, in 1894, the Army FA affiliated with the Football Association. Numerous photographic postcards of these military elevens survive, with the season, regiment, or battalion, often chalked on the ball, the uniformed officers posing stiffly alongside the players.

Postcards are frequently found of teams based on places of work: factories, utilities, railways, post offices; whilst others defy any categorisation – 'Ye Old Crocks, Tenterden, April 9th 1913', presenting a group of Kentish stalwarts of doubtful vintage, photographed at their big match.

Before the Great War, people not only played football in their hundreds of thousands, but also flocked in droves to the leading venues to watch their soccer heroes. Attendances had increased steadily during the 1880s and 1890s, with aggregate totals for League matches increasing from 600,000 (12 clubs) in 1888-9 to 1,900,000 (16 Div. I clubs) in 1895-6. The FA Cup final of 1901 attracted the first 100,000 gate, to see Tottenham and Sheffield United play a drawn game at the Crystal Palace, but even this figure was surpassed in 1913 when over 120,000 converged on South London to watch the final between Aston Villa and Sunderland. League matches had meanwhile continued to attract the masses, with over 5 million watching the games of 20 First Division clubs during the 1905-6 season.

The onlookers usually paid 6d (2½p) to stand on primitive terracing, or a little more to sit on wooden benches in roughly constructed stands. Most of the grounds had started life modestly as enclosed fields, with later piece-meal modifications, although clubs such as Everton, Aston Villa and Newcastle United boasted splendid stadia. Manchester United did not play their first League game at Old Trafford until 1910, when they lost to Lancastrian rivals Liverpool, and Woolwich Arsenal played south of the Thames until 1913.

Many postcards were issued of the crowds, the grounds, and the matches in progress. We have already recalled the activities of the Brighton brothers, Tom and G. A. Wiles, photographing the spectators at the Goldstone Ground before and after the First World War, when Brightonians were able to purchase post-card mementos of their visits to the games. A similar service was offered along the coast at Portsmouth where Stephen Cribb snapped various sections of the Fratton Park crowd during the FA Cup game in 1911, when Pompey were easily defeated by Aston Villa. One speculates however, whether the Hampshire fans were over keen to acquire photographic reminders. Most of these crowd scenes were the products of local photographers, although it has already been noted that W. H. Smith & Son published a card framing part of the huge congregation witnessing the 1901 FA Cup final on the Crystal Palace ground.

Postcards of football games in progress were popular with pre-First World War fans, and cards of a particular match could be on sale locally within a few days of the event. A particularly fine series of cards was issued by J. Taylor of Byker, and captures several incidents from the FA Cup semi-final at Anfield in 1908, when Newcastle swamped Second Division Fulham by six goals to nil. Two of the goals are recorded thus: "Caught Napping" by Rutherford'; and "Netted" by Howie'. Taylor became a touch more shutter-shy in the final though, when the Wolves overcame Newcastle by three goals to one. The final of 1911 also involved Newcastle, this time against Bradford City. The game required a replay at Old Trafford, with the Yorkshiremen winning by the only goal. A photographic card of the telling strike taken from behind the Stretford goal is captioned 'Cup Final At Manchester. "The Winning Goal". "Who Got That Goal?"' The doubt reflecting uncertainty at the time, as to whether the scorer was O'Rourke or Spiers.

The international match between Scotland and England on 4 April 1908, at Hampden Park, Glasgow, established a new attendance record, with an esti-

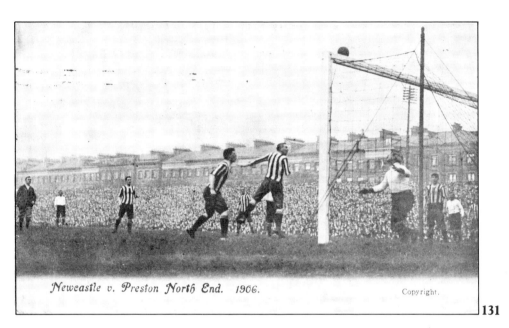

Newcastle v. Preston North End. 1906.

Copyright.

131

POT-POURRI

A CORNER KICK

WATFORD DRAW WITH LEYTON 2-2. FEB 6TH 1909.

132

CUP TIE. FRATTON PARK. 1911. POMPEY V VILLA. 14.
S CRIBB. PHOTO.

13

ALBION Y SWINDON HOVE 1913.

13

THE UMPIRE
The Best
Weekly Paper
for
General News
and Sport.

Reproduced from
THE UMPIRE
of Nov. 8, 1903.

G.E.T.

W. LEES (BARNSLEY).

135

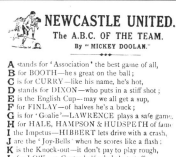

NEWCASTLE UNITED.
The A.B.C. OF THE TEAM.
By "MICKEY DOOLAN."

A stands for 'Association' the best game of all,
B for BOOTH—he s great on the ball;
C is for CURRY—like his name, he's hot,
D stands for DIXON—who puts in a stiff shot ;
E is the English Cup—may we all get a sup,
F for FINLAY—of halves he's a buck ;
G is for 'Goalie'—LAWRENCE plays a safe game.
H for HALE, HAMPSON & HUDSPETH of fame
I the Impetus—HIBBERT lets drive with a crash,
J are the 'Joy-Bells' when he scores like a flash ;
K is the Knock-out—it don't pay to play rough,
L for LOW – a Centre half who's hot stuff ;
M is our MAC. a hard nut to Crack(en),
N for NEWCASTLE—our boys never slacken ;
O is the 'Opportunist' which all like to see,
P is for Pugnacious —likewise Penalty ;
Q is the 'Queue' lined up for the fun,
R for 'ROBBI' and RAMSAY who centre on the run
S is for 'Shoot' when HENDERSON lets fly,
T is the 'Thrill' when COOPER dashes by ;
U for 'UNITY'—it helps on the team,
V is Cup 'Victory' of which we all like to dream ;
W the 'Whistle' some Refs play a lot,
X is the 'Xcellence' of Secretary WATT ;
Y are the 'Yells' which help players along,
Z is the 'Zest' that we sing the old song,

"PLAY UP UNITED."

Copyright. Published by Benton & Co., North Road, Brighton.

136

Swindon 1
Manchester 0
United

In Memory of

MANCHESTER
UNITED
WHO FELL, FIGHTING FOR THE
ENGLISH CUP,
(First Round)
At County Ground, Swindon.
JANUARY 10TH, 1914.

Manchester United
Didn't want to die,
They didn't want to do it
There was a reason why,
But Swindon had to kill them
(It may have been a sin),
They really didn't want to,
But they did want to win.

A.A.

137

"Jimmy Lawrence"

138

POST CARD.

The address to be written here

CRYSTAL PALACE

Apl 28/10

Ye Beggor'
W've got ye
at last!

Mawson, Swan & Morgan Ltd., Newcastle-upon-Tyne.

Mr Fred Foulds Junr

Mapplewell Rd

Woodhouse Eaves

Nr Leicester

Leicestershire

141

BRIGHTON & HOVE ALBION'S MASCOT BULL-DOG "ROSE"

142

—A FAMOUS DEFENCE—
HOLDSWORTH, STIFFY & McCALL

143

Play up Manchester United!

Just signed on

1

WELSH FUSILIERS 1913. No.1.

1

94

146

147

148

14[

150

15[

152

96

131 'Newcastle v Preston North End. 1906' – uncredited publisher. The Lancastrian masters of the 1880s battle with the Edwardian aristocrats.

132 Downer Photo – 'Watford Draw with Leyton 2–2, Feb 8th 1908'.

133 S. Cribb, Photo, Portsmouth – 'Cup Tie, Fratton Park, 1911. Pompey v Villa'. Not Pompey's day, Villa scoring four goals to Portsmouth's one.

134 T. W. S. Wiles, Hove – 'Albion v Swindon. Hove. 1913' Each of these crowd photographs was numbered for identification and purchase for the family album.

135 Reproduced from *The Umpire* – '"Umpire" favourites. W. Lees (Barnsley)'.

136 Benton & Co, Brighton – 'Newcastle United. The A.B.C. of the Team'. A little versifying . . .

137 . . . and a little Hearsifying.

138 '"Jimmy" Lawrence'. Uncredited publisher. The Newcastle goalkeeper, from a series of caricatures of that excellent pre-First World War side.

139 Brown and Bernard Ltd – 'Come on Everton, Just Room for You'. A pugnacious Crystal Palace await Everton in the 1906–7 FA Cup competition, having already disposed of Newcastle, Fulham and Brentford.

140 H. J. Fletcher, Barnsley – The tombstones carry epitaphs to Barnsley's 1910 FA Cup victims. The empty grave awaits Newcastle but the Colliers had dug their own plot. The Magpies won the replayed final 2–0 on Everton's ground.

141 Mawson, Swan & Morgan Ltd, Newcastle – 'Aprl 28/10. Ye Beggar We've got ye at Last'. A contented Magpie – after losing the three previous finals, the Cup resides finally in his nest.

142 T. W. S. Wiles, Hove – 'Brighton & Hove Albion's Mascot Bull-dog Rose'. Dogged defence?

143 Ralph & Co, Preston – 'A Famous Defence – Holdsworth, Stiffy & McCall'. Comedian Harry Weldon and two 'stooges' from his 'Stiffy the goalkeeper' musical hall routine.

144 Aristophot Co Ltd – 'Play up Manchester United. Just Signed On'. Move over Meredith! Postally used 1911.

145 The Bournemouth View Co Ltd – 'Welsh Fusiliers 1913'. Military football has a long history. The Royal Engineers of Chatham were losing finalists in the first FA Cup tournament, an Army Cup was contested in 1888–9 and in January 1894 the Army FA affiliated to the Football Association.

146 Private photographic postcard *c*1905. Lack of playing facilities hindered the early expansion of working-class football. This game is being played through the efforts of groups like the Manchester and Salford Playing Fields Society (1907) and other similar organisations throughout the country.

147 Private photographic postcard *c*1910.

148 'The Hanneford' West Penwith Perpetual Junior Football Cup, value £25.

149 'Garratt Lane Mission Football Club. Winners of Wandsworth Auxiliary League,

1908-9'. Uncredited photographic postcard. The link between religious organisations and athletic sports is well documented. Aston Villa, Barnsley and Everton inter alia emerged via the Victorian dog-collar.

150 Marshall, Keene & Co, Holborn – 'Football Group. Craven College, Beckenham 1911-12'. In the twenty years before 1900, school football became increasingly structured, with Schools' Football Associations established in South London (1885), Manchester (1890) and Leeds (1896). The Edwardian years saw the formation of the English Schools Football Association (1904).

151 'Who said we didn't win the cup?'. Private photographic postcard. Distaff United shoulder-to-shoulder? c1910.

152 Ridley's Studios, Tenterden – 'Ye Old Crocks', Tenterden, April 9th 1913.

mated 120,000–130,000 fans paying £7,000. The game ended in a draw at one goal each, and the Dundee publisher, Valentine, issued souvenir cards showing football action and the vast crowd. Scotland lost the 1909 contest, played in England, but gained revenge in 1910 when another 100,000 crowd saw Scotland to victory by two goals to nil. This time the Glasgow publisher, Potter & Co, produced postcard souvenirs to commemorate their nation's triumph.

The Rotary Photo Company issued a number of photographic cards in a series titled 'London Life'. Football was considered worthy of inclusion in this keenly collected set, and the card numbered 10513–70 is captioned 'London Life. Football, Chelsea v Aston Villa At Stamford Bridge'. A sub-caption advises purchasers of the ever increasing popularity of the game in the capital city.

Alongside the pills and potions dispensed by Boots Cash Chemists was a series of 'Real Photographic' postcards, including one of 'Woolwich v Sheffield Wednesday'. No further identification is offered on the card, although the action is from the FA Cup semi-final of 1907, when the Owls beat Woolwich Arsenal and progressed to meet Everton in the final, where Sheffield took the trophy.

Not all the action cards were of these important Cup and international matches. Less elevated competition was on view from non-League games; ordinary League matches; and Southern League action, such as Watford's encounter with Bristol Rovers on 5 October 1907, when the Rovers inflicted a home defeat on Watford by two goals to one. The Hertfordshire photographer, Downer, was on hand to photograph the unfortunate event for a postcard issued in a series covering various Watford games during 1907–8.

The football grounds themselves attracted the attention of several postcard publishers, Aston Villa's stadium receiving more recognition than most. Valentine issued an early collotype card of the Villa Park ground, cheekily modifying one of the advertising hoardings to read 'Valentine's Picture Post-cards'. The former Villa player and photographer, Albert Wilkes, produced a panoramic shot of the arena, taken from a lofty vantage-point, and the London publishers, Birn Brothers, in their 'B.B. Series 62', issued a poor quality coloured card of Villa's ground.

Sheffield Wednesday's palatial home was of more modest pretentions in 1904, as evidenced by a card posted in October of that year, and sold in the 'Royal York Series' by W. H. Smith & Son of Sheffield. Special events such as the opening of a ground, naturally invited the publishing of commemorative cards, and this was indeed the case in Middlesbrough with a 'Souvenir of the Official Opening of Ayresome Park, Saturday, September 12th, 1903'.

The sporting press was well established by 1900; the most authoritative voice of football, the *Athletic News*, first appeared in 1875, and by Edwardian times was published weekly in Manchester, giving full reports of all the important football, rugby, cricket, cycling and athletic events. The Saturday football specials had been published since the 1880s, and most local newspapers gave generous coverage to footballing matters. During the early years, photographic illustrations were few and usually of poor quality, but the sports cartoon had developed into an art-form in its own right.

The *Kentish Independent* followed Woolwich Arsenal's progress during 1904-5, the club's first season in Division I, and commented on the previous week's game, aided by an ingenious and lively cartoon. The South London publisher, Molyneux, issued a series of thirty of these drawings, reproduced on postcards; including one of a momentous day, when the Gunners blasted 26 goals past shell-shocked French opposition. Several facsimiles of these early Woolwich cards were recently re-issued by Islington Libraries.

Arnold Bennett's hero, Denry Machin, in *The Card* (1910), recognised the advantages of being involved with the local football club, in furthering his political ambitions. Football was a useful metaphor in communicating political ideas, and its propagandist value was to be exploited later, during war-time. Raphael Tuck published a series of cards on 'Fiscal Football', in which the artist P. V. Bradshaw, employed football symbolism to illustrate Joseph Chamberlain's protective trade tariffs. As Tory Secretary of State for the Colonies, he believed that keeping foreign goods at bay would help to strengthen the Empire. In 'A Good Piece of Headwork', Chamberlain is seen defending his 'goal' of protectionism against an attack of menacing imports. Other cards in the set find Chamberlain in similarly uncompromising mood.

Product advertising often seeks to associate well known celebrities with the peerless merchandise. It is not unexpected then, to find 'Oxo' linking itself with the sinewy athleticism of football. Postcards, from their earliest days, had proved a useful and cheap means of promoting a product or company, and football cards were no exception. Portsmouth and Crystal Palace had both averred on pictorial cards, their indebtedness to the beefy cubes, and the two 1904 FA Cup finalists, Manchester City and Bolton Wanderers, appeared on a matching pair of 'Oxo' postcards. The famous London store, Gamages, sought to advertise its sporting goods, via an early 'write-away' postcard of a spindly artist-drawn footballer, who looked incapable of lacing his own boots, and himself in need of a sizeable quaff of Oxo's potent brew.

It was as dispensers of a different brew that many superannuated footballers lived out their days. The public houses were an early focus of football activity, and even after the turn of the century, some professional clubs claimed them as headquarters, with mine host often an ex-player himself.

A postcard published about 1905 by J. Sharples of Marple prints the caption 'Headquarters Manchester United FC'. The card shows the façade of the building, and the image of a player in United colours, with his name, Harry Stafford. Geoffrey Green has written that 'a statue should be raised to him outside the Old Trafford of today'. No statue has yet been raised, but the Imperial Hotel still stands near Manchester's Piccadilly Station.

In 1902, Newton Heath FC were in dire financial trouble, so much so that the creditors foreclosed. A shareholders' meeting in March heard that the FA had agreed to a reconstituting of the club, but that £2,000 was needed. Harry Stafford, the club captain, amazed the gathering by announcing that he knew four men each prepared to invest £500, as he himself was. The club became known as Manchester United, ousting rival suggestions, Manchester Celtic and Manchester Central. One of the saviours, J. H. Davies, became the president, and was said to have met Stafford through the player's Saint Bernard dog. At a bazaar, held in 1901 to raise money for the club, the owner and dog became separated. An employee of Davies found the animal, which was returned to the player, who later sold it to the businessman for his daughter. The crucial introduction had been made thanks to the four-footed go-between, and the expiring football club resuscitated.

The football writer, Ivan Sharpe, believed the years 1900 to 1914, to have been the golden age of the game. Safety play, he claimed, had not arrived, and teams went out to attack. Others may demur at his sentiments on the game as played. What is without question, is the fact that these years were the golden days of the postcard publishers, when their salesmen most definitely went out to attack. The postcard photographers, artists, designers, and publishers, conspired to create a uniquely rich and varied series of graphic images and attitudes to soccer, that captured the era, just as cigarette cards were to characterise the inter-war years, and video recordings, the 1980s. Although the war in 1914 boosted the sales of many types of postcards, most football cards either passed away or went into hibernation until the cessation, whence they emerged as feeble and emasculated shadows of their former selves.

On this gloomy and funereal note, we end our survey of pre-First World War soccer postcards with mention of the *in memoriam* card. Its heart-rending dirge and anguished pain of defeat, are dedicated to losers everywhere.

Boldly to the fray we went,
On honour, fame, and vict'ry bent;
But with sad hearts we came away,
For the match we'd lost today.

Our opponents they were far too good;
In fact we stood like logs of wood;
Our chance is past, our day is o'er,
At football we will play no more.
R.I.P.

WAR AND THE DOLDRUMS

Figures issued by the Postmaster General in his annual reports, show that the numbers of all postcards mailed including both plain official Post Office cards and privately printed pictorial ones, increased steadily each year until 1913. That year a slight decrease was recorded, although in 1914, the upward trend seemed to continue, with an increase of 27 million on the previous year. In 1915, though, the figure of 880 million, was over 46 million down on the total of the year before. The impact of the war was certainly responsible for this huge reduction, when perhaps the frivolity of a pictorial greetings card or whimsical cartoon became suddenly out of place in the new climate.

The postcard, however, quickly adapted itself to war conditions, with a whole new range of war-related themes: naval battles, destruction, fund-raising, patriotism, propaganda, etc. Postcards were also quick and convenient ways of sending messages from the scene of action to families at home. Although statistics are not available for the years 1914–1918, it is likely that more postcards were sent during the First World War, than at any other time.

The postcard Golden Age is thus generally considered to extend from 1900 until the cessation of hostilities, when sales suffered a more permanent reduction. The football postcards with which this book is chiefly concerned, belong, however, to those years before that fateful day in June 1914, when Gavrilo Princip gunned down the Archduke Franz Ferdinand. Soccer postcards were certainly far fewer in number after the outbreak of war, but they did not disappear totally.

The First World War
The season 1914–15 was a much troubled one for the football authorities. The major competitions continued as in peace-time, but the clubs suffered the problem of falling attendances caused by the war. In October 1914, the clubs of the Football League agreed to contribute $2\frac{1}{2}\%$ of their gross receipts to a fund for helping their poorer members, and the players also donated a percentage of their wages.

As well as financial difficulties, the game had to defend itself against critics who claimed that it was hindering recruitment. In November 1914, the FA Council responded by asserting that upwards of 100,000 recruits had been enlisted from football, exceeding the combined totals of all other sports. The Council went on to point out that all the professional players of the leading clubs underwent weekly military drill, with rifle ranges also installed in most modern grounds.

The directors of some clubs stated that they would have been happy for a ban on football, but had to continue, because they were contract-bound to the players. One director, in a letter to the *Times*, felt that a large percentage of spectators at football matches were either soldiers, or workers in vital industries,

102

and that only a small fraction of fans attending the games were eligible for recruitment.

Football came under relentless attack from newspaper editors, as did other sports, including horse racing. The Hon George Lambton, on behalf of the equestrian fraternity, suggested that one could not compare football with racing. Jockeys, he said, were small men, whereas footballers were strong athletes who should be soldiers. Horses, he also argued, were vital to continue the line of English thoroughbreds. He did not, however, draw the inference that footballers should also be protected for stud, to continue the line of English sinew. The newspapers were not sufficiently impressed with football's justifications, and in late November, the Council of the Newspaper Proprietors' Federation of the London dailies resolved to carry no more than the barest match results.

Football continued with its normal programme until the spring of 1915. The FA Cup final was won by Sheffield United, who defeated Chelsea in front of 50,000 at Manchester, and the League Championship went to Everton, just ahead of Oldham Athletic. A 'Footballers' Battalion' of the Middlesex Regiment had already been formed, including players from Clapton Orient, Plymouth, Nottingham Forest, Fulham, West Ham and Reading.

In July 1915, a meeting in Blackpool, of the Football League, Southern League, Scottish League, and Irish League, agreed that 'the best interests of the nation and those engaged in the war and preparing the munitions of war, will be best served by the continuance of football'. However, the various leagues were to approach their national associations to discontinue the registration of professionals. All professional players were henceforth to revert to amateur status. The Football League Management Committee recommended that 'in view of the pressing need for recruits and workers . . . and in the hope that every eligible young man will find in the service of the nation a higher call than the playing of football, the League competition for next season should not be proceeded with.'

The Football and Southern League competitions were not resumed until the 1919–20 season, although various of the leading clubs arranged their own regional leagues known respectively as the London Combination, The Lancashire Section, and the Midland Section. No medals or trophies were to be awarded, and games had to be played at approved times.

Few, if any, postcards of the clubs playing in the war-time leagues were issued by the major postcard publishers, although occasionally one-off photographic cards of these war-league clubs are found, players often guesting for the club local to their army camp, or place of work.

Not surprisingly, the most frequently discovered cards of this period are of military teams. Most regiments could boast former League and even international footballers, and a match for example, between Lancashire and Yorkshire soldiers in the 1916–17 season, involved players, all of whom had been with First or Second Division League teams before the war.

One 'cup final' not found in the record books was played during the early days of the war at the Ruhleben prison camp. Steve Bloomer was coaching in Germany on the outbreak of war, and found himself interned at Ruhleben where he helped 'Tottenham' win the final of a series of games at the camp. Newcastle's Edwin Dutton, also played for the Spurs in the final against Oldham Athletic, who fielded a 'scratch team of public school boys'. Everton's success with the high balls must have been limited – they were represented by jockeys interned at Berlin's Hoppergarten. A rare photographic postcard exists of Bloomer at Ruhleben. Taken towards the end of the war, it shows him posing with team mates before his last game there. After the war he coached in Holland, Canada and Spain.

The propaganda value of the postcard in war-time was soon seized upon. Football imagery was part of the vernacular, and served as a useful medium to engender popular feelings and attitudes. One card, titled 'A Miskick', shows a Teutonic soldier attempting an almighty boot at a football, missing the ball completely, and ending up flat on his back. 'Dis vos a sure goal. Just votch me.' – 'Mit vun kicks I.' – 'Donner und blitzen!'

Although the war ended in 1918, the FA and league representatives agreed that no FA Cup nor full international games should be played during the 1918-19 season. A number of 'Victory' games were played however, Chelsea beating Fulham by three goals to nil in the London Combination Victory Cup final at Highbury in April 1919, and during the same month, England drew 2-2 with Scotland in a Victory International played in Liverpool. The football programme proper got underway on 30 August 1919, when the first League games were played after an interval of four years.

The Inter-War Years

Writers on matters deltiological have divided the various postcard epochs according to key dates. The 'early period' is usually considered to extend from 1870, when the first plain official Post Office card was issued in Britain, to 1899, when the authorities acceded to the larger size UPU card. The Golden Age spanned the years 1900-1918, when postcard popularity was at its height. The inter-war years witnessed a decline in both quantity and standards, and Anthony Byatt, in *Collecting Picture Postcards – An Introduction*, has quaintly dubbed this nadir, the 'Doldrums'.

By 1930 only half the immediate pre-war number of cards were sent through the post, the usual explanations offered for this lessening of interest, include the doubling of the inland rate from ½d to 1d in June 1918, and a general waning of enthusiasm. Increased costs meant that the publishers were no longer able to reproduce the fine quality printing of earlier days, and so the cards themselves may have proved less appealing.

The postcard publishers were certainly mindful of the effects of the increased postal rate, when a proposed (and temporarily implemented) further increase was

153

154

WORLD WAR I
TO WORLD CUP WILLIE

155

156

157

~ BRIGHTON & HOVE ALBION ~
CENTRE~FORWARD.

~ IRISH INTERNATIONAL ~
SEASONS ~1920~21 AND 1921~22.

J. DORAN, BRIGHTON'S GOAL SHOOTING CENTRE~FORWARD

G.A.WILES
BRIGHTON.

160

161

162

163

164

165

166

167

FOOTBALL
CUP FINAL

OFFICIAL
Souvenir Postcards
OF
To=day's Teams
AND
Stadium.

6D.
PER PACKET

Printed by *Fleetway Press Ltd*   Published by CAMPBELL GRAY, Ltd., London, W.1.

THE STADIUM~BRITISH EMPIRE EXHIBITION WEMBLEY

COPYRIGHT

CAMPBELL-GRAY L⊺ᴰ LONDON.W.

THE F.A. CUP FINAL — BOLTON WANDERERS

NUTTALL   HOWARTH   ROWLEY   SEDDON   PYM   JENNING   FINNEY
    BUTLER   JACK   J.R. SMITH   JOE. SMITH   VIZARD

170

THE F.A. CUP FINAL — WEST HAM FOOTBALL TEAM.

MR KING   W. HENDERSON   S. BISHOP   G. KAY   A.E. HUFTON   J. YOUNG   J. TRESADERN   C. PAYNTER
(SECRETARY)   (TRAINER)
        R. RICHARDS   W. BROWN   V. WATSON   W. MOORE   J. RUFFELL

171

Wolverhampton Wanderers Football Club

Season 1930-31.

172

HULL CITY CUP TEAM. 1930.

174

CLAPTON ORIENT F.C. 1935-36.

DERBY COUNTY F.C. 1935-36.

NEWCASTLE UNITED F.C.

176

T. FINNEY.

177

STANLEY MATTHEWS

178

111

ESPAÑA 82

Naranjito ™

179

WORLD CUP WILLIE

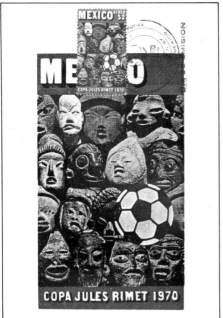

181

153 The War Cartoon Studios – 'A Hot Time for "The Hun's Goal!"'

154 'Southport Central 1916–17'. Wartime competition Lancashire Section. Top row (left to right): Dorward, Corporal Rigby, Schofield, Stringfellow, Hamer (dir), Clayton (sec), Corporal Toms, Fearns (trainer). Bottom row (left to right): Merritt, Caulfield, Watson, Corporal Abrams, Corporal Campbell, Wright, Rimmer.

155 J. Salmon, Sevenoaks – 'Goal!' After F. G. Lewin.

156 'Military Match at Manchester: The Lancashire Team'. Standing (left to right): Gunner Broad, Gunner Eccleston, Bombardier Lees (sec P.N.E.), Gunner Sutcliffe, Gunner Kellock, Gunner Cook, Gunner Bullen, Gunner Kelly, Gunner Swarbrick. Seated: Gunner Barnes, Bombardier Boyle, Gunner Speak, Lt Shepherd, Gunner Latheron, Gunner Walmsley, Sergeant Tootel. Played 1916–17.

157 C. E. Willis – 'D. Jack'. FA Cup winner's medals with Bolton Wanderers and Arsenal. An English international who played in the first Wembley FA Cup final.

158 Brighton Camera Exchange – 'B & H Albion Cup-Tie Team 1924. Brighton v Barnsley'.

159 G. A. Wiles, Brighton – 'J. Doran, Brighton's Goal Shooting Centre-Forward'.

160 P. O. Collier, Reading – 'Reading FC. Players 1919-20'.

161 Albert Wilkes, Photo – 'Arsenal Football Club, Season 1920-21'.

162 W. E. Turton, Huddersfield – 'Huddersfield Town AFC 1921-22'. The footballing masters of the 1920s. Herbert Chapman's Huddersfield posing with the FA Cup (1922). They were League Champions in 1924, 1925, 1926 as well as finishing runners-up in 1927 and 1928.

163 G. S. Ellis, Mansfield – 'Mansfield Town FC 1923'.

164 Hepworth Photo, Bristol – 'Bristol Rovers Football Team. 1923-24'.

165 Crawford Photo – 'Tottenham Hotspur FC. 1924-5'.

166 Carbonara Co, Liverpool – 'Liverpool Football Club. 1926-1927'.

167 W. Whiffin Photo, Poplar – 'Millwall FC. 1927-8'.

168 Cambell Gray Ltd, London – Official Souvenir Postcards. Wembley's inaugural FA Cup final inspired these postcard offerings. Not Golden Age standard but all the same, a pictorial record of a historical event.

169 Cambell Gray Ltd, London – 'The Stadium – British Empire Exhibition Wembley'.

170 Cambell Gray Ltd, London – 'The FA Cup Final – Bolton Wanderers'.

171 Cambell Gray Ltd, London – 'The FA Cup Final – West Ham Football Team'.

172 Poulton Bros, Wolverhampton – 'Wolverhampton Wanderers Football Club Season 1930-31'.

173 W. H. Duncan, Hull – 'Hull City Cup Team, 1930'.

174 R. Mason Photo, Clapton – 'Clapton Orient FC. 1935-36'.

175 W. W. Winter Photo, Derby – 'Derby County FC. 1935–36'.

176 'Newcastle United FC FA Cup Finalists – 1951'. (Left to right, front row): Walker, Taylor, Milburn, Robledo, Mitchell. (Left to right, back row): Cowell, Harvey, Brennan, Fairbrother, Corbett, Crowe. It was no small compliment to Newcastle that their less youthful followers, compared the sides of the early 1950s with their Edwardian antecedents.

177 Valentine & Sons Ltd, Real Photo Football Personalities series. R.P.69 – 'T. Finney'. *c*1954.

178 'Stanley Matthews'. Published 1951. Drawing after McNamara.

179 'España 82'.

180 'World Cup Willie'. The 'swinging sixties'; Carnaby Street the hub of the Universe and Hungary '53 exorcised as England beat the World.

181 'Mexico Copa Jules Rimet 1970'.

182 Veldale (Limited Edition of 1,500) – 'Bulldog Bobby'.

suggested in 1921. A battery of letters from several leading publishers bombarded the Postmaster General, pleading with him to reconsider the decision to raise the rate from 1d to 1½d. They predicted disaster for the industry, and the charge was indeed reduced again the following year, after their successful campaign. Despite their success, sales still declined during the 1920s, and the 1930s became an era of drab sepia views and gaudy, tasteless, seaside humour.

The Inter-War Years

Association Football resumed its normal activities after the war, with West Bromwich Albion winning the 1919–20 First Division Championship, and Aston Villa, the FA Cup. Villa's defeated opponents were Huddersfield Town, a team that was to dominate the 1920s under the managership of Herbert Chapman. In pre-war days, the Southern League was a powerful competition, but in 1920 its First Division clubs applied *en masse* to the Football League, being accepted as Associate Members in a new Third Division. The League acquired a Third Division (North) the following season, Stockport County, its first winners.

Picture postcards of football teams and players still appeared during the 1920s and 1930s but the main publishers were largely noticeable in the soccer arena, by their absence. Most of the team line-ups were the products of local photographers and publishers, and several of their names were mentioned in an earlier section. Brighton was well represented in the 1920s by G. A. Wiles and the Brighton Camera Exchange, Millwall by cards of W. Whiffen of Poplar, Tottenham by W. Crawford of Edmonton, Bradford City by Walter Scott, and Brentford by Wakefield of Ealing. Huddersfield Town, who won the League Championship three years in succession in 1924, 1925 and 1926, were recorded by W. E. Turton, who also produced portrait cards of the individual players. Amateur and 'fun' players were photographed for the family album, and these cards, excellent period-pieces, survive in huge numbers.

The one event during the 1920s demanding a special souvenir, was the historic first FA Cup final at Wembley Stadium in 1923. An official souvenir set of three cards was indeed issued; one card of the stadium, and one each of the two finalists, Bolton Wanderers and West Ham United.

The numbers of humorous, artistic and 'miscellaneous' football cards of the 1920s are small compared with the Golden Age bounty, but a few are nevertheless found. The artist Fred Spurgin produced a series of cards of '20s flappers for the Art and Humour Publishing Company, in which these female footballers appear in a number of disruptive and distracting situations: 'Playing the Game with the Boys' (768), 'Making Up for the Otter Players' (769), 'The Girls are Soft on a Football Player' (776), and similar. The Photochrom Company issued an unusual set of six cards in the mid-1920s, silhouetting various artist-designed football incidents.

Soccer postcards of the 1930s are not plentiful. This was a time when the cigarette card and magazine give-away had ousted postcards as collectable items of football memorabilia; 'got any fag cards mister?' was the catch-phrase then. The 1930s belonged to Arsenal as the 1920s belonged to Huddersfield. They won the FA Cup in 1930 and 1936, and the League in 1931, 1933, 1934, 1935 and 1938. Arsenal's giants of this period were on sale from the photographer Lambert Jackson of Holloway Arcade, London N7. The Gunners' team groups portray a 'Who's Who' of 1930s football, with stars such as: Bastin, Compton, Copping, Drake, James and Male, appearing on a postcard of the 1936 team posed with the FA Cup.

Although cards of the 1930s are in the main, traditionally grouped team line-ups, the occasional 'special' stands out. When the Wolves reached the final of the FA Cup in 1939, a replica of a vertical montage with players in oval insets, first issued for the 1908 final, was published, replacing the old Wolves with their latter-day descendants. Unfortunately this attractive souvenir is a reminder of failure. The Midlanders were heavily defeated by Portsmouth.

This was the last final before the outbreak of the Second World War. The main football competitions were abandoned on the outbreak of hostilities with only a few games of the new season played, although a series of regional leagues was instituted. The FA Cup was not competed for again until the 1945–46 season, and the League programme not resumed until 1946.

TO WORLD CUP WILLIE AND BEYOND

The pictorial football postcard waxed with the new century, declined during the 1920s, and limped through the 1930s. Its flame was, however, never totally extinguished, and examples from the decades since the Second World War serve to provide a semblance of continuity from those vintage days of the early Edwardian collotype vignettes.

By the 1950s the firm of Valentine & Sons had been producing picture post-cards for over half a century, including, as we have already noted, a series of fine artist-designed souvenirs of leading early-century English and Scottish teams. Cards of footballers had been largely ignored by the giants of postcard publishing since before the Great War, but in the early 1950s, this Scottish company turned back the clock. The mellow sepia and warm colour printing of earlier times, were replaced by a harsh photographic black and white; austere, and characteristic of these post-war years. Valentine's 'Real Photo Football Person-alities Series' features Stanley Matthews and Tom Finney, those two touch-stones of English football, whose adulation passed beyond simple hero-worship to near deification. Joining Matthews and Finney in the series are: Jimmy Dickenson, Billy Wright, Ronnie Allen, Gilbert Merrick, and Ivor Broadis.

Another publisher active during the Golden Age, and still printing cards after the Second World War, was Gladstone Adams of Whitley Bay. Adams was a local photographer, and his name has already been mentioned alongside the Newcastle United players of their pre-First World War hey-day. The 1950s were also bountiful years for Newcastle, winning the FA Cup in 1951, 1952 and 1955. This same firm issued a series of photographic cards of the 1952–3 Geordies, just as they had of their Edwardian antecedents. The 1951 FA Cup final between Newcastle and Blackpool was the excuse for a pair of souvenir postcards of the two finalists, issued in conjunction with the *Daily Herald* news-paper. This final had most neutrals wishing a winner's medal to Stanley Matthews, although the trophy did not go to Lancashire, but to the North-East. The old maestro did however, finally pocket his gold two years later, in 1953's emotional game.

The 1950s were a low point in the history of English soccer. The self-delusion of England's supposed global footballing superiority, was glaringly exposed at Wembley in 1953, when the Hungarians taught the national team a lesson by 6 goals to 3. England's first contact with the World Cup was in 1950, when they were humiliated by the USA. It was in February 1958 at Munich, that Manchester United's blackest chapter was penned, when Duncan Edwards and friends were tragically taken, returning from a European Cup game in Belgrade.

The gloom of England's failures on the ever expanding world soccer stage was dispelled in 1966 when an affable, leonine mascot – World Cup Willie – saw the host nation take the Jules Rimet Cup in extra-time at Wembley. There were many souvenirs of that tournament, and a coloured postcard of Willie from the Photographic Greeting Card Company must have been one of the humbler, but evocative today nonetheless. The 1960s were years of British optimism; when the axis of the Earth shot through Carnaby Street, the Beatles ruled the airwaves, and England were surely fated to emerge football masters of the world. The abolition of the maximum wage in 1961 enabled the better players to increase their earnings, shed the cloth-cap, open boutiques and encamp in stockbroker land; soccer became show-biz.

Football is an ephemeral occupation, and thumbing through a series of coloured postcards by Coffer of London, underlines how the 1970s hero quickly becomes 1980s sober-suited manager. Joe Royle of Everton, David Webb of Chelsea and Alan Mullery of Spurs, all then at the peak of their playing careers, have since taken the manager's role. The Newcastle team of 1969–70, line-up with the Inter-Cities Fairs Cup which they won in 1969; and the fine Manchester City team, coached by Malcolm Allison, includes Colin Bell, Mike Summerbee and Francis Lee, all England internationals.

Recent years have seen a revival of creative, colourful, finely printed postcards. Social commentary, biting political satire, current events and innocent recreations have all found expression on a new generation of cards worthy of purchase and preservation. The 1982 World Cup tournament in Spain produced many excellent cards from several countries. The host nation adopted a smiling citrus fruit 'Naranjito', as its national mascot, and he duly appeared on a series of eight welcoming postcards from Spain. England opted for a ferocious, growling 'Bulldog Bobby' to symbolise its approach to the matches, although the team eventually proved shot-shy and toothless. Veldale, one of the publishers of the 'new movement', issued a 1,500 limited edition card of mascot Bobby, titled 'Spain '82'.

Of more novelty than aesthetic appeal are cards from Fisa (Great Britain) and J. Arthur Dixon. The latter producing a series of postcards displaying the emblems of well known clubs, the crests removable and carrying adhesive backs. Fisa's cards eschew the rectangular shape in favour of a circular 'football', whose panels frame views of the teams' grounds. Manchester United and Liverpool are two of these 'rounded' teams.

Most leading football clubs now claim their souvenir shops, with whole tempting catalogues of team memorabilia. Alongside the hats, scarves, books, ceramics, towels and video recordings, the simple picture postcard may today plead the poor relation, but its pedigree is nevertheless, long, worthy and venerable.

118

APPENDIX I
SHORT GLOSSARY OF POSTCARD TERMS

The revival of interest in collecting old postcards has generated and re-discovered a specialist jargon, of which several instances have been employed in this book. A few of these terms are outlined here.

CARTOLOGIST Postcard collector. Rival term to 'deltiologist'.

CHROMOLITHOGRAPHY A printing process for colour reproduction in which various colours were separately applied via stone blocks.

COLLOTYPE A printing technique which does not break up the image into dots, as in half-tone, but uses a gelatin-treated plate to react to the tonal variations of the original. The result is smoother than the half-tone, giving better definition.

DELTIOLOGIST Postcard collector. From the Greek *deltos* (writing-tablet).

DIVIDED BACK A card with the back divided into 'message' and 'address' halves. Approved by the Postmaster General in 1902, F. Hartmann produced the first such card that year, and a d.b. card of the 1902-3 Portsmouth team by this publisher must be one of the earliest such football cards.

HALF-TONE A print on which the tone is reproduced by the variation in size and density of dots. This pattern is achieved by photographing the original through a mesh called a half-tone screen. The result can lead to a loss in definition unless the dots are small and the spacial density high.

LOCAL PUBLISHER A publisher whose cards were only of interest in the immediate vicinity, rather than of more general appeal. Many football cards fall into this category, often the products of local photographers selling their photographs in postcard format.

MONTAGE The result of 'mounting' several separate elements to produce a composite whole. A popular technique was to create a football team design from photographs of the individual players, using head-and-shoulder portraits set in circular or oval frames.

REAL PHOTOGRAPHIC A postcard on which the image is a direct photographic print on light-sensitive paper. Provided there has been no fading, this type of card offers the most detailed and realistic reproduction.

UNDIVIDED BACK A postcard on which the whole of the back was given over to the address, any message having to vie with the illustration for space on the front (see 'Divided Back'). It cannot be concluded that no u.b. cards were used after 1902. Old habits die hard, and old stock takes time to sell.

VIGNETTE The 'undivided back' postcard compelled the message to cohabit on the front of the card with the picture. The illustration was perforce a vignette fading away to blank space. In some instances the subject occupied less than half the available space, whilst in others an 'encroaching' vignette just left an exaggerated border.

WRITE-AWAY A device in which the opening line of the prospective message was printed on the card, often a pun on the accompanying illustration. Raphael Tuck issued a 'Write-Away' series, although other publishers also employed the style. Tuck's title has been accepted as generic by latter-day collectors. 'I tried hard to drop across you . . .', as a bulky footballer flattens a slim-line opponent.

APPENDIX II
SELECTED DATES AND EVENTS

1863 Inaugural meeting and founding of FA on 26 October.

1869 World's first postcard issued by Austria on 1 October.

1870 Britain's first official postcard issued on 1 October.

1871 FA Challenge Cup instituted.

1872 Privately printed cards permitted, although still requiring an official embossed stamp. First recognised England v Scotland international. First FA Cup final played on 16 March at the Oval.

1885 Professionalism conceded by FA.

1888 Football League formed.

1889 Preston North End won League and FA Cup.

1890 Irish League formed. Scottish League formed.

1892 Second Division added to Football League.

1894 Privately printed postcards with separately affixed stamp accepted on 1 September. Southern League formed.

1895 First FA Cup final played at Crystal Palace. First official 'court size' postcard.

1897 Message no longer excluded from address side, although uncertainty not clarified until 1902. Aston Villa won League and FA Cup.

1899 Larger Universal Postal Union size cards accepted by Postmaster General.

1901 First attendance over 100,000 saw Tottenham and Sheffield United play FA Cup final at Crystal Palace.

1902 Divided back postcard accepted by Postmaster General. Collapse of stand in Glasgow during Scotland v England match, causing many deaths and injuries.

1904 Formation of FIFA.

1905 In February, Middlesbrough paid Sunderland £1,000 for the transfer of Alf Common.

1907 Amateur Football Association founded following break-away from FA of several leading amateur clubs.

1908 England won Olympic Games football competition in London.

1909 Threatened strike over the FA's refusal to accept the Players' Union affiliating with Federation of Trades Unions.

1911 FA Cup replaced by new design from Fattorini and Sons of Bradford – the third trophy. Bradford City kept the 'pot' in Yorkshire by beating Newcastle in the final.

1912 England won Olympic Games football competition in Sweden.

1913 Aston Villa and Sunderland played FA Cup final before 120,000 at Crystal Palace.

1914 Last FA Cup final at Crystal Palace. Burnley won the game, witnessed by King George V. Britain entered war 4 August.

1915 Regular League and Cup competitions suspended for duration of the war. 'Footballers' Battalion' formed.

1918 Postcard rate doubled from ½d to 1d on 3 June.